Heartfelt Leadership

*Nine principles to sort your team,
work and life*

Kerry Swan

A catalogue record for this book is available from the National Library of Australia

ISBN: 978-1-922553-78-2

Printed in Australia by McPherson's Printing
Project management and text design by Publish Central
Cover design by Pipeline Design

The paper this book is printed on is certified as environmentally friendly.

Disclaimer
The material in this publication is of the nature of general comment only, and does not represent professional advice. It is not intended to provide specific guidance for particular circumstances and it should not be relied on as the basis for any decision to take action or not take action on any matter which it covers. Readers should obtain professional advice where appropriate, before making any such decision. To the maximum extent permitted by law, the author and publisher disclaim all responsibility and liability to any person, arising directly or indirectly from any person taking or not taking action based on the information in this publication.

To my dear friend Sandy.
Thank you for holding up the mirror to show me
the possibilities of heartfelt leadership.

A book for you

If you are a senior leader …

- with a lukewarm team

- who is struggling to get the right things done

- and you are not quite sure about where to go next, or if you are on the right track

… then this is a book for you.

If you are an intelligent leader …

- who is bloody good at your job

- who wants direct, no-nonsense advice

- who needs to think both practically and strategically

… then this is the book for you.

Heartfelt Leadership is a practical leadership book that will help you solve problems at work, address issues with your team, sort out problems with different personalities and devise strategies. It is also a philosophical book, and it will help you fix the most profound stuff and the most important stuff so that you can truly live the life that you want, when you are ready.

Contents

Introduction

When I started writing this book, I thought it was going to be easy. *Heartfelt Leadership* was going to be a book about leadership for women. Strong, smart women. Women who are leaders, but who, like you, are looking for something more.

But then I realised that this book is also about men. Empathetic, strategic men. Men who know there must be a better way to lead. Men who, like you, can feel the difference between effective and unproductive leadership. So *Heartfelt Leadership* became a practical book. A book that's equally important for the blokes.

This book is not about how women are better at support than men. And, it's not a book about blokes being better at outcomes. This book is about balance and, most importantly, courage – because it takes courage and a deep sense of balance to be a heartfelt leader.

When Viktor Frankl, Holocaust survivor, psychologist and author, wrote his book *Man's Search for Meaning*, he did not distinguish between men and women; but rather focused on the courageous choices they made. Courageous choices about self-determination and personal leadership in the most trying of conditions.

And, when Brené Brown, university researcher and author, embarked on her career exploring courage, vulnerability and shame, she did not distinguish between men and women in her work; instead, she chose discomfort over control.

While working as a coach, entrepreneur and leader, I have learned that leadership, especially personal leadership, requires daily doses of courage. You need to check in both with your heart and your head, make the big decisions, make the right decisions and then leap into action.

THE TROUBLE WITH LEADERSHIP

Along your journey, you might have noticed that the leadership style that you have adopted is not getting the results you want. You may have found that hard logic and results are features of your adopted leadership style. Likely, this style doesn't feel empathetic or kind to the people around you.

Or perhaps you have found that you still have issues with your team, no matter what you do or how nice and patient you are. You are not getting the traction you need to deliver results.

In my experience, this kind of discovery starts around the middle of your career. You begin to question your leadership life with its endless list of tasks, people and problems to deal with. Or, more specifically, you may be struggling with things like:

- getting your team members to do what you want while still having a good relationship with them
- identifying the best strategic approach or solution to a particular business problem
- the existential questions that arise mid-career, such as,

'Is this what I want to be doing? Or, if I want to be doing something different, am I brave enough to make that jump?'

You might have even attended some training or some professional development along the way to try to 'fix yourself'.

If you, like my clients, are asking yourself these questions, know this: you can think more deeply about your approach to leadership, and you can change.

I would go as far as to ask you if, in your current leadership approach, you are being true to yourself? Indeed, it is these types of questions that signal you are ready to consciously start creating the leader you want to be.

I hope that *Heartfelt Leadership* will help you to choose a more balanced approach to leadership. Because heartfelt leadership is about two things: fixing work, people and team problems, and then understanding the deeper reasons why you have the issues in the first place.

Heartfelt Leadership will teach you how to lead others and lead them the way they want to be led.

Heartfelt Leadership will also help you get clear about what you want in your life. It will help you manage and embrace times of chaos. Adopting heartfelt leadership will set you and your team up for high levels of accountability and teach you the importance of difficult conversations. You will understand the language of heartfelt leaders and focus on the brevity of life to make sure that your legacy lives on.

WHO AM I?

I am Kerry Swan. I am a recovering hard-arse, a project manager by trade and a lifelong achiever.

Along my journey, I transitioned from a sensitive and creative child to a young woman who believed in the dream: the dream that I could have it all. The dream that I could have it all, as long as I played by the masculine rules of leadership. These were the rules in the 1980s workplace that included winning at all costs; rules that rewarded outcomes and results; and rules that meant you had to be tough. Rules that meant that my focus became tasks and getting things done to become a leader.

Later, when I was a single mum, these rules were further enforced by the patriarchy. I had something to prove, and I wanted to prove that I could do it all. I could be the protector, the provider, the nurturer and the support all rolled into one. These were the years of no mercy and getting the job done at all costs.

Luckily for me, around seven years ago, my great mate Sandy held up a mirror and asked me who I was. (I'll tell you the full story of her intervention in principle 3.) She also asked me 'Why?' Why was I on a relentless quest to be right and to win at all costs? And, why did it matter so much? At this moment, my transition to a heartfelt leader began. It's a journey that I've lived while writing this book.

My entrepreneurial and creative streak fights for attention with my known and well-worn command-and-control skill set these days. It is a battle that I struggle with – every day.

Thankfully, writing this book has set me free.

It has set me free to find the courage to be a heartfelt leader.

These days, I am on a quest to find a more authentic approach to leadership and find the right skills for now.

But my journey in heartfelt leadership is a work-in-progress, and yours will be too. Being a heartfelt leader is not about getting there, hitting the goal and reaching the milestone – it is about the journey. That's the difference between heartfelt leaders and the rest. We celebrate the journey.

A HEARTFELT LEADERSHIP MODEL

Have you naturally drifted into leadership rather than it being a goal you aimed for? Perhaps you are a leader because you are good at your job? Or maybe you have a knack for convincing other people to follow you? Either way, many of us become leaders without a whole lot of conscious choice. It just happens.

As a leader, you might have adopted the leadership principles of the people who have led you. Perhaps you haven't given much thought to whether those principles are relevant to you. Or perhaps those adopted principles don't feel right anymore.

For too long, the world has adopted a masculine approach to leadership – leadership that is heavy on logic, mathematics and results. The heartfelt leadership model challenges this approach and proposes that if you want to lead people and projects to success, you need to reorient your leadership to a more balanced perspective.

The heartfelt leadership model is about making a conscious choice to adopt a more poised style of leadership. It is about challenging past tenets of leadership. It is also about skill sets. I will call them 'heartfelt skill sets' and explain them as I move through the book.

I will also argue that traditional leadership models have overlooked the importance of our feminine skill sets in leadership settings, and I will explain my thinking on this.

With a more balanced and courageous approach, the heartfelt leadership model will help you get more done with less stress regarding your people and projects. It will also support you in creating real change with less hassle from your team.

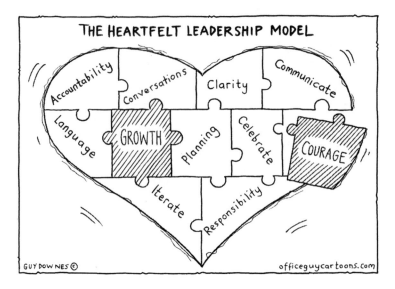

The heartfelt leadership model is based on nine principles. These nine principles have helped me, and the people that I have coached, over many years. The nine principles offer you a roadmap out of your day-to-day management pain and into a more courageous style of decision-making and leadership.

The nine principles do not need to be approached in a linear fashion (although it can help). They can be used in a standalone manner to help you solve immediate problems. But if you put them together and practise them regularly I promise you will see a change in your team, your work and your life.

Heartfelt leadership does not ask you to give up your existing leadership skills. It also does not make your current approach wrong. Heartfelt leadership encourages you to add to your leadership tool kit with heartfelt skill sets.

Heartfelt skill sets are sets of two complementary but opposite energies – masculine and feminine – which together deliver real change.

By mindfully combining your masculine energies (like logic, structure and order) together with your feminine energies (like empathy, creativity and innovation) you will begin to deliver a more effective approach to leadership.

And with this more mindful approach, the heartfelt leadership model will help you develop your own unique and contemporary style of leadership as you engage the balancing energies of the heartfelt skill sets.

As well as stepping you through the nine principles and their complementary heartfelt skill sets in detail, I will also give you some very practical activities that you can implement straight away.

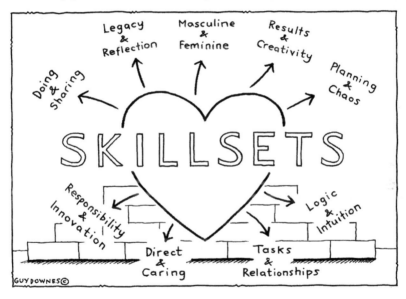

Simply put, heartfelt leadership is a new model of influence based on courage and growth, not command and control.

Our workplaces, teams, families and communities are made up of both men and women. And they need heartfelt leaders: leaders who can balance results with creativity. Leaders who lean into chaos and relationships while still getting the job and the tasks done. Leaders who can deliver direct and useful feedback in an empathetic and caring manner. Leaders who will hold us all responsible while encouraging innovation. Leaders who work with us to create a lasting legacy, while reflecting on our growth.

If you are a leader in your business, family or community, I want to help you to enhance your leadership in a balanced and heartfelt way. Stick with me through the nine principles, and I will take you on a fun and practical exploration of how you can be a better leader – every day.

1

Get clear about what you want

Life is short. You have a finite amount of time to create change.

And, because life is short, you need to make good decisions on where you want to invest your precious energy. Simply, this first principle is about getting clear about what you want – and what you want to achieve. At work. At home. In life.

Principle 1 asks the real question of you, as a leader – what do you want to be remembered for? What creation, what result, what relationship or change do you want to effect?

To live your truth as a leader, you must get clear and focused about where you are going and why.

But, to live your truth as a heartfelt leader, you need to tune into both your creative (feminine) skill set and your results (masculine) skill set. By getting both creative AND results-focused, you are more likely to create a more meaningful and rich life.

Covid-19 has taught us how fragile life is, and how tenuous our jobs, health and economies are. It has allowed us to reflect.

Personally, as a recovering hard-arse project manager, my career, to date, has been all about the task. I have not focused on the journey or the relationships that I have made along the way. One person who has been a significant influence on me has been my best mate, Sandy – a relationship-driven friend who lived from her heart.

During my 30s and 40s, I was lucky to have Sandy as a friend who reshaped my thinking about leadership. She was heart-driven where I was logic-driven. She was creative where I was task-focused. Sandy held up a mirror to me and taught me about personal leadership. I'd love to share some of that learning with you throughout this book.

This principle focuses on the problem. You might have been so focused on getting a good job, marrying, raising kids or getting the next promotion that you have built a safety net or a cage of comfort around yourself, and you don't know what to do next.

In this chapter, I will help you get clear about what you want. I will ask you to engage your dreams (creativity) and then, and only then, assess them for action (results).

Today, there are so many choices, and you don't want to lose what you've built by making a mistake. I want to introduce the first principle in the heartfelt leadership model, which is the most critical bit – getting clear about what you want. And, in this principle you will deploy a little bit of feminine-based creativity to get the ideas rolling. You will then balance it out with a little bit of old-fashioned masculine planning to make it all happen.

CREATIVITY: YOUR LIFE ENERGY

KEEP CREATIVITY AT THE HEART OF EVERYTHING YOU DO.

, ıııance Hu.
Logistics Procure
Marketing Public Rela
Strategy Supply Chair,
esearch & Development
Funding Cash flow
Systems **CREATIVITY**
Machinery Sales Customer
Distribution Staffing
Recruitment Operations
'earning Crisis managemen
rses Leadership Supp'
Management Ir
Social Re-
Hor'

Community.
Data Culture Le.
Sourcing Reward Prc
Planning Implementatio.
Human Resources Custc
Salaries Information T
Facilitie'
Service Fee'
Change Plannin
Values F

GUY DOWNES ©   officeguycartoons.com

You are overwhelmed with choice in the modern world. Study. Don't study. Work. Don't work. Career choices: endless. Job opportunities: unlimited.

But it doesn't matter which road you take as long as it is one that you choose.

1990s and divorce

Back in the 1990s, when I was a baby in the workplace, I honestly bought the story that I could have it all – careers plus babies plus life. Fast forward 20 years, I now know that you can have it all at a cost. For me, that cost was my first marriage and my health at the time. At the age of 38, I found myself a single mum with a business to run and what I call a large STD – sexually transmitted debt. I was a slow learner, and I found that getting clear about what I want has helped me create the relationship I want, the business I want and my chosen lifestyle. It took me about ten years, but I'm on track to living a life of my own choice these days.

Ultimately, you will never know about the other road because you didn't take it. You will never know what would have happened *if*. *If* you had taken that job. *If* you had started a business.

So, why not create a life of your design and your own choice, and then consciously create and tune into your heart about what it is that makes you happy?

Once you have identified what you truly want and it is something that makes your heart sing, then and only then should you put a magic ruler of logic across your dream.

And, when you put the magic ruler of logic across it, you should be asking yourself, '*How* shall I get to this new world?' rather than using your logic to determine that it is too hard, it is too big, it is too scary, and convincing yourself against it.

Simply put, if you don't know what you want, you will end up living someone else's life. Someone else will decide what's good for you.

I'd much rather you have the freedom to choose your road.

I get that you might be concerned about wanting to leave your options open. 'What if things change or what if something new happens?' you might ask.

Getting clear about what you want helps you plan things, explain them to your team and lead the change. You can constantly adjust along the way.

I want to clarify that I'm not talking about throwing it all in and changing careers or husbands (although this has been done) in a midlife crisis. I'm talking about listening closely to your heart and getting clear about what kind of life you truly want.

Activity 1: 'My best life' journal

One of the simplest ways to get creative and think about what you want is to simply take some time out and go for a walk in nature or sit in the park for an hour. The change of scenery will help your mind to wander and consider your options. You won't get creative when sitting in front of your phone, your computer or a spreadsheet for hours on end.

When you are out on that walk, breathe deeply and let it all go. I want you to breathe so deeply that your heart can feel it. Breathe in deeply so that your back expands and your shoulders lift back. Hold it for a second, and then breathe out, picturing your breath leaving your body through your heart. I know that you breathe out through your nose/mouth, but I want you to picture breathing out through your heart. Feel your heart relax as your breath moves out of your body.

When you are out walking, try to distract yourself from the surroundings and relax. You might even find that when you are out walking, and the less you are trying, the more creative you will get because your brain is free to run around and explore. For some people, the same thing happens in the shower. You are more creative in the shower because you are not in 'work mode'.

In this more relaxed state, I ask you to consider what your best life would look like, what you would do if you could and what is possible. Let the answers come, but don't judge them yet.

When you do get home or back to work, then and only then, do some of the practical stuff and write your thoughts and plans down in a journal or a digital file.

When you are getting creative, you might find that you come up against your self-doubt, which makes you nervous about what you might like to do. Nerves are a good thing; they tell you that the idea is exciting.

If you are feeling a little anxious, I encourage you to increase your clarity, visualise the future, increase the details and the picture of what your new life or strategy might look like. Get clear in your mind about what you want by detailing what your best life might look like, how it might feel, who you might be, where you might live and what you might do. The clearer you can describe that, the more likely you're to realise your best life as a possibility.

He's just not that into you

Back when I was single, the universe tested me in lots of ways. And one of them was the parade of suitors who thought they might like to get to know me. It was quite the circus with multiple married men, teenage boys and single women all letting me know, in different ways, they were available. But, you know, not available in the true sense – available in a complicated, messy, uncomfortable sense. I am sure that it was the universe asking me to get clear about what I wanted. Around that time, I read *He's Just Not That Into You* by Greg Behrendt and Liz Tuccillo. It was full of sage advice encouraging smart women to stop wasting their time agonising over mixed messages. It must have hit a nerve because it motivated me to clarify what I wanted in a relationship. I still have that book, and inside the front cover I listed my requirements for a new man. I slept with the book by my bed for a couple of years. Not so long later, the love of my life stumbled into my world. At our first interview (date), it was clear that he ticked all of my boxes. And, as a bonus, my dog liked him. A lot.

So whether it is pursuing a new relationship, getting clear about your career or simply what to do with a tricky business problem, I encourage you to tackle this first activity as if your life depends on it. Because it does. Too often, we make logical decisions based on fear or discomfort, rather than what we know to be right in our hearts. Embrace your creativity. Consider what you want. Ask yourself, 'What life do I want to lead?' Because there is no escaping. As Paulo Coelho says in *The Alchemist,* 'You will never be able to escape from your heart. So it's better to listen to what it has to say.' Pursuing our unique personal mission is the most important thing that any of us can do.

RESULTS: YOUR LIFE EFFORT

Having a dream is a great place to start.

I want to talk about your masculine skill set and, in particular, your results focus and what you use to get things done.

When you clarify your focus, it helps you to get things done. The alternative to being focused is trying to be everything to everyone, and you end up helping no-one.

The only one who can

I'm right in the middle of setting up our new company, an earth-moving business, and hand on heart, I can tell you that old habits die hard. Part of the start-up process was to create a work health and safety system for the whole business. It's a mountain of work that I committed to doing when I was trying to do everything else everywhere else as well. I had a bunch of other work better suited to my skill set and more aligned to my life goals, but I chose to tackle work health and safety because I lacked the creativity and courage to find a better way.

The sheer volume of work, policies, systems and effort led to me crying at my desk on a Sunday afternoon because it was just all too much. I had fallen into the trap of saying, 'I am the only one who can do this. There's nobody else possibly in this universe who can help me with this.' I had fallen into a task-based decision and logic trap.

Of course, other ways and other people could have helped, supported and done the work, but my ego and the need to please meant that I spent most of my Sundays in summer writing health and safety policies. This self-appointed martyrdom gets stuff done, but it doesn't advance my progress as a heartfelt leader.

As a heartfelt leader, you need to focus on what you want, rather than volunteering or saying yes to please everybody. Indeed, the job needs to get done, but the real question is, what is the best way to get it done? This is where your creativity matters.

A life lesson like this will tend to come around repeatedly. You might not catch the lesson the first time, but I guarantee the lesson will come round and round in your next iterations. But more about that later.

Edith Eger, author of *The Choice*, is an Auschwitz survivor. She went on to become a psychotherapist and has written two books. She contends that we all have a choice about how we will live our lives in every moment.

You might be worried what happens if you change your life and back the wrong option, and then change your mind and do something different. Or, even worse, what if you fail? It's a pretty common objection and doubt. But there's no such thing as failure; there's only learning. It's how we perceive the process rather than how we label the process.

Don't be cruel to yourself or others. We are all entitled to our own choices, and you should never negate other people's choices. Just because I might want to be a superstar in my field, that doesn't mean that's what other people want to do – because that is their choice. Life and leadership are all about respecting other people's choices.

Activity 2: Weighing up your options

In activity 1, you free-formed and brainstormed your best life. And I hope that you got creative and in touch with your feminine skills and explored all sorts of possibilities and found some things that scared you a little.

Now you are going to shift gears. You will now adopt some of your masculine energy and start to get focused on the results.

You can let a little logic and some details and practicalities creep in here. But don't entirely lose your creativity yet!

I would like you to now write up all your options into a list and add a couple of columns headed up 'pros' and 'cons'. It might look something like this:

Changing jobs during the Covid-19 pandemic

Options	Pros	Cons
Move to Sydney	Better money Metropolitan lifestyle	Current epicentre of Covid Cost
Start my own business	More freedom Legacy for my children	Risky trading conditions Finance required
Apply for a promotion	Familiar with the company Known performer	Not stretching myself Industry is slowing

Activity 2 engages your creativity (by designing the life you want) and your logic (by getting results-focused). It will help you to reach a sound decision about which option is going to best move your life forward with the resources that you have available.

Holiday decisions

When Covid-19 arrived in Australia in 2020, I worked in my own business as a real estate agent. A significant part of that business was our holiday rent roll. Over the course of two weeks, when the first Australian lockdown happened, we took about 100 cancellations resulting in the loss of around $300,000 in revenue. It was a challenging and scary time. I didn't know if we could sustain our business, and no-one had any idea how long lockdown would last. I thought that I would be terminating staff and closing the business.

Early in this process, I worked with my team in crisis mode. But, as the days turned into weeks, we saw signs of recovery and managed to hold on. Restrictions lifted, South Australians began to travel intra-state and our business began to recover. But, I can tell you, this kind of roller-coaster leaves scars.

Over the next 12 months, we had many conversations about the long-term viability of this holiday rental business. We even considered closing down due to the volatility of the market with ongoing border closures.

Earlier this year, my team and I weighed up our options, just like I asked you to do in activity 2. We applied some creativity in terms of what we wanted our life (post-Covid) to look like and applied some logic to determine our results. The outcome? A profitable new business model that delivers better results than our pre-Covid approach.

RESULTS: FEAR-DRIVEN DECISIONS

During my real estate days, I was selling a business for a client, and he was goal-focused and clear about what he wanted, which was good. He was ready to move on to a new project, but he decided that the buyer I was presenting was out to get him. He put up all manner of resistance and a stack of objections to the sale. Eventually, I said to him, 'What's going on here? Who do you think the buyer is?' Then he told me who he thought the buyer was, which was so far from the truth. He had created a story in his head about who he considered the buyer was and felt that buyer was going to buy him out so he could laugh at him. His emotions were screwing with his results. He was allowing the emotional feedback that he was getting to upset his results because we were talking about two different people.

When he realised the buyer wasn't who he thought it was, he calmed down and was much happier to work his way through the process. He realised it was simply a deal that we had to get done, and he was okay. We were able to move forward and look at the outcomes of that deal. This tale is a cautionary one that says, 'Here's where sometimes we can allow our emotions to make fools of ourselves, rather than using them as guidance.' Our emotions should be used for guidance rather than making solid, logical, rational decisions.

You don't want to compromise your results by making reactive and emotional decisions. You should use your emotions and feminine skill set as an early warning trigger to tell you what's going on and seek evidence. It's part of that masculine and feminine balance that we're aiming to achieve.

Working with women over the years, I've seen many of us make our decisions based on assumptions because we're reacting from an emotional standpoint. I'm encouraging you to use that emotional, early warning sign as a trigger to go and check the facts.

You might believe that you are not emotional at work. You might also think that you are entirely logical and factual in your decision-making. I want to debunk the idea that emotions are always extreme – crying and being upset and angry about things. Sometimes it's just thinking, 'I don't feel like I like that person,' or 'I don't feel comfortable with this decision.' Every minute of the day, you make decisions emotionally about how you feel about a person, about a situation, about a scenario. Then you justify them logically with, 'Here's the evidence that that person's no good.'

I want to be clear that emotions are not destructive. They're simply an indicator of progress, and you should listen to them. You don't need to shut them down and become unemotional; you need to use them as an early warning trigger.

Activity 3: Assess options logically, but link them to the big picture

In any decision, there needs to be a strategic return on investment in your long-term future that is beyond (but including) the money. You might ask yourself whether your return on investment could be:

- financial

- emotional

- physical

- mental

- time and lifestyle-based.

Using the previous example of changing jobs during Covid-19, your preference might be to start a business. The freedom of business appeals to your bigger-picture life goals, but now you want to assess it logically. You might use a framework like this:

Return on investment – starting a business

Financially	Short-term cash requirements will lead to greater financial security for my children
Emotionally	Increases my self-belief and confidence
Physically	No more two-hour commute to work
Mentally	It sets me up with a challenge to grow my skills
Time and lifestyle	After an initial start-up phase, my lifestyle will be more flexible due to the business model that I want to create

AN EARTHMOVING BUSINESS

My husband and I bought an earthmoving business about a year ago as I write this section. With his background in contracting and mine in project management, it was a logical purchase. At the time of purchase, we assessed the financial return and naively the time that we thought it might take to reorient the business. And while I would like to say we carefully evaluated the return on investment for us emotionally and mentally, I would be lying. The purchase was way bigger than either of us anticipated and had a lot more financial, mental, physical, emotional and lifestyle costs than expected. But, along the way, this assessment technique has helped us realign our vision on tough days. We need to stop to take a breath and reflect that the long-term payoff and alignment to our big goals means that the return on investment is there for both of us.

CONCLUSION

How you choose to invest your life energy matters, because you can end up spending too much time living someone else's life. As a heartfelt leader, you get to consciously choose your life direction and where you're going to put your effort. Our lives will change when we get results-focused on what matters to us and our loved ones.

I'm sure that your life is pretty good right now. It's pleasant. It's fun. It's maybe even just a little bit boring. You need to challenge yourself to step outside of your comfort zone and get a little bit of help to make something real, exciting and new happen. You – and only you – are in charge of your destiny. This responsibility is as frightening as hell, but stick at it and see what happens.

You will only get the life you want if you take the time to dream a little, logically assess your options and then jump off the metaphorical cliff.

To get clear about where you're going and stop doing what you don't like, you will need to deploy both your feminine creativity and your masculine results orientation.

Life is about to get crazy. Before the dawn of a new day, you're going to need to face the dark night of your soul.

2

Work backwards

I hope that principle 1 made you a little uncomfortable about making a change and living the life you want. Principle 2 is about the importance of planning and how a little chaos in our lives makes for much more fun and better projects and people.

How are your New Year's resolutions going? Remember them? Resolutions to get fitter, not take any crap, not eat any crap, start a book or change a job?

Likely, by around January 15, you have forgotten those resolutions in the busyness of your modern life.

In reality, making lasting change is tough:

- Life gets in the way.

- It's messy, complicated and human.

- When you start, you think you can control change.

- You also honestly believe that things will happen exactly as you want them to.

- They won't – you will get sick, tired and busy along the way.

But! There is hope. 'Change is hard at first, messy in the middle and gorgeous at the end' as author and leadership expert Robin Sharma reminds us.

A heartfelt leader knows this. They plan for the best but expect chaos and make necessary adjustments along the way.

Conventional leadership wisdom suggests that a strong and good leader creates everyday habits to make sure things happen. Or, as the planners amongst us believe, that good leadership is all about planning.

Covid-19 taught us something very different. In reality, as a heartfelt leader, you need the flexibility to consider that things change. Hearts change. Minds change. Our environment changes.

Critically, we all have a heart. And a heart is an emotionally driven animal that loves to react to the chaos.

The secret to being a heartfelt leader is that if you actively anticipate heart-driven chaos during your planning process, you are more likely to succeed as a leader of people and projects.

HEALTH AND MY BODY

I know firsthand that you will make yourself sick if you think you can control everything and everyone. It's impossible. The universe doesn't work like this. Over the last ten years – I am a slow learner – I have seen evidence that my health has been compromised when trying to control everything. Like the time when I was 40 years old and came down with glandular fever, which, ironically, is a young person's disease. I attempted to keep working, but eventually, my body gave up when my liver was compromised, and I had about ten weeks on the couch, followed by six months of recovery.

More recently, my upper body gave me the early warning signs of being out of whack with discharge coming from my breasts and a breast cancer scare – again, at a time when I was attempting to control the speed and pace of the world.

Even during Covid, when the pace of my life was simpler but my business world was collapsing, my body let me know that I couldn't control everything. I developed a bunch of feet and hand allergies that eventually culminated in a sore back. That's a complicated story, but they were warning signs that said, 'You cannot control the outcome of everything.'

Every single time I'm going too hard or in the wrong direction and trying to control the outcome, my health is compromised.

Adopting a heartfelt leadership approach will allow you to plan for the best-case scenario that rolls with the realities of life.

During my life as a project manager, I learned that in an ideal and perfect world, I need to make project plans, strategic plans and business plans. And, I honestly trusted that everything would go according to those plans. The reality was very different.

Most projects and plans come unstuck because you cannot control humans, suppliers, the economy or the various moving parts of a project. This is not to say that you should not have a plan. Rather, I am saying the opposite. You *must* have a plan. And you *must* expect that chaos will cause you to adjust your plan.

As a heartfelt leader, I continue to invest my time and energy in planning, but I also know that I live day-to-day with varying degrees of chaos and uncertainty. Things will go wrong.

Planning gives us structure and certainty; life gives us learning.

THE IMPORTANCE OF PLANNING

Just a heads up – I'm a project manager by trade. I live for Post-it notes and schedules. I can teach you how to chuck anything into a workable plan. I'll make it visual, and I'll explain it, so it doesn't overwhelm you. When we're done you'll have the steps, the chunks and the timeframes worked out. This approach to planning will make you feel safer, more organised, and clear. For the control freaks and those playing along at home, put your hands up: this will make sense and feel good. Getting clear about the stages and phases of a project is a critical step if you are leading a team.

Project planning might seem obvious, but it's an essential part of working out where you're going. If you can't map out where you're going, how the hell do you expect your team to follow?

Moving offices

Back in my admin days, I organised an office move well before I started in project management. Like lots of projects do, it began as a conversation in the tea room. My boss said to me, 'All right, Kerry. You're our organiser. Would you organise the office move?' I said, 'Yeah, sure. I'd love to do that.' Within about three minutes, I was back at my desk, opening up an Excel chart and planning all the steps to move the office from here to there. I had scant information about the scope of that project. I bustled along and started organising the move – the Telstra phone line changeover, the boxes and getting people to pack up their stuff, and so forth.

About two weeks later, after I'd costed it, scheduled it and made it all happen – I'd booked the trades and suppliers, and so forth – I was in the same tea room, and my boss said, 'How are you going with that office move?' I said, 'I'm going great. I've done this,

I've done this, and I've done this. We're all on track, and we're all ready to go.' He replied, 'What about the other site office? Have you included them in the move?' I said, 'No. We didn't talk about the other office.' He said, 'Well, you're going to need to include the other office.' So I slammed off back to my desk because I had to rewrite the whole project, rewrite the budget, rewrite the schedule, rewrite the bookings and rewrite the quotes.

I had not planned the office move very well. I had made my decisions based on many assumptions. This, in my experience as a project manager, is how most projects start. They start at the water cooler, finish at the water cooler, or end at the pub down the road where somebody is traumatised because they've had such a bad journey.

Project planning is like oxygen for us as leaders. The better we can get at project planning, the better chance we have of leading our people and our projects efficiently so that we all enjoy life and work a little more. The same goes for making changes to your leadership style.

Project planning works equally well when you are making a change at home or changing your lifestyle. Project planning works any time you need to engage the people around you and get them on board with any change or move you want to make.

Maybe you think that you don't have time for that because it's all about getting started and going straight into implementation in the workplace. There's generally not enough time to pause and plan. But, to quote a founding father of the United States, Benjamin Franklin, 'If you're failing to plan, you're planning to fail.' I want to share how we can do it together, map out your ideas, and get them on paper at a high level.

Activity 4: Post-it note planning

I am a born-and-bred project manager at my core. But, this book isn't a book on project management. There's a whole other body of evidence to explore if you're interested in knowing more about project management. Here, I'd just like to share some basic planning techniques to help you out with this particular process of making changes in your life.

Back in principle 1, we covered how to get clear about what you want. The important thing here is to be clear in a detailed and visual way. For example, if you're going to change your job, get clear about the result – 'I want to change my job' – and what your life might look like when you do. You might have shortened your commute time, or you've got better pay or more responsibility.

When you're clear about the change that you wish to see, grab yourself a bunch of Post-it notes – this is my favourite bit – and then write on those Post-it notes every thought, task or action that you will need to do to support changing your job and all the things that you need to do to change your career.

For example, you could write, 'I need to update my résumé,' 'I need to go and talk to some recruiters,' 'I need to get my LinkedIn profile up-to-date.' All of those things that you need to do to make that change go onto a Post-it note. Brainstorm it all. Don't think about it too much and don't correct it. Just get them all down. Once you've exhausted that, start putting those Post-it notes up on a big wall and begin to sort them into logical groups.

Those logical groups might be:

- Writing tasks: I need to write a résumé. I need to write my LinkedIn profile. I need to write a cover letter.

- Research tasks: I need to go to various places and search for information about a new job.

- Shopping tasks: I need to get myself an interview suit. I need an interview folder. I need to get myself some new shoes.

Sort them out into their logical groups and put them into what I call chunks. Have a heading for each of those groups. When you've got those headings sorted out, you're able to shift them into stages, phases and chunks. You might choose to do these tasks in an order that makes sense logically to you. When you've got your primary timeframe sorted out, you can start to write on your Post-it note how long each task will take. How long will it take me to go shopping? How long will it take me to do the research? How long will it take me to write?

You might be worried that you're going to get confused or too bogged down in the details or minutiae. Take a breath and get somebody else to help you with it – maybe somebody who is detail-oriented or likes playing Tetris – because sometimes we're too close to our subject.

Stay tuned for the next step in the process in activity 5.

PLANNING SMALL STEPS EVERY DAY

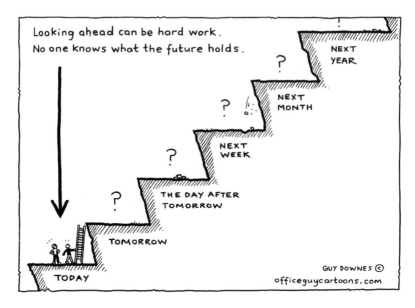

Your journey is made up of small steps that matter every day, not just one big jump. It's cliché to say this, but Rome wasn't built in a day – though the Romans were undoubtedly laying bricks every hour.

Writing a book

I chose to write this book during possibly the busiest phase of my life. As I explained earlier, we have recently purchased an earth-moving business, Covid-19 has impacted my real estate business, and I have all the usual family and community demands like you. To think that I could write a book and manage not only the earth-moving and real estate parts of my life, but also work inside our agribusiness and oversee a family property portfolio, was nothing short of insanity. But there you go. Small chunks of time applied consistently meant that I was able to create this piece of work.

It is consistent daily effort and focus that get you results, not a big monumental sprint or a marathon.

You might make a New Year's resolution that you will get fit, and you are going to be lean and buff by February. The result of this will most likely be disappointment. But if you're persistent and do a little bit every day over 12 months, you will find that muscle building happens with small improvements every day. Any skill development that you undertake will happen slowly. You're not likely to be perfect on the first day just because you desire it.

You might decide that you're going to get bored while learning your new skill on your journey. If this is the case, go back to principle 1, work out why you started in the first place and remind yourself of your goal, sharpen your whole picture of the future and keep your mind focused on where you want to go.

And, like in project management, you might find that you're on the wrong path and have made the wrong choice. That's okay. It's all about learning. You can go back, look at your Post-it notes, change them and restart or reorient the process.

Activity 5: Organising your Post-it notes

Now it's time to take the chunks of information that you described in activity 4 and start to fill out the details. For each one of those Post-it notes, detail who's going to do what. For example, updating your LinkedIn profile or résumé – who's going to do that for you? Are you going to do that? Are you going to get somebody else to do that? When will they do that? How long will it take for them to do that? Is there any cost attached to that?

Once you've worked your way through each one of those little

Post-it notes, you have a detailed framework of the small steps that you need to take. It's not as overwhelming as 'I'm going to find a new job.' It's about the little steps that you need to take to find a new job.

Fun fact: this is the process that we use to create a work breakdown structure – a project-management technique that the best project managers use, whether building a submarine or a playground. You're halfway to being a project manager and having a happier life, which is more important.

You might identify yourself as a strategic thinker and find this task too small. Alternatively, you might identify yourself as a details thinker and not see it big enough to get the results that you want. Get some help from your team, your mentor, your leader, your subject expert. Ask them to review it.

PLANNING – WHAT DO I NEED TO LEARN ON MY JOURNEY?

If you need to make a significant change, you won't be an expert in your new world. You'll need a plan about what you need to learn along the way.

To make a change, you're going to need to change. The best thing to do is to plan for that, which will make it more likely to happen.

Brendon Burchard is a high-performance coach and one of the highest-performing speakers on personal development in the land. He talks about how we need to have structure for our growth. If you're not making the time in your diary to learn new stuff, you're not going to learn new stuff. He explicitly asks to see your diary and where you're reserving time to get that LinkedIn profile updated or get your résumé updated.

You might be thinking, 'I don't know where to start, so I don't know what I don't know. I don't know yet how to start looking for a job.' Nothing hurts us when asking a good question. Find people and ask them how they made the change. How did they get a new job? Where did they find the connections? Where did they find the job? How did they go about updating their résumé and LinkedIn profile? What else did they do to improve their online presence? What were the things that they did that made them successful in getting a new job?

This plan is not about creating a learning and development plan for you; it's a strategy for what you need to do to get yourself ready for the life you want. It would be best if you didn't feel like you have to change everything. You might have to tweak two or three things.

In principle 1, we talked about getting clear about where you're going. In principle 2, we've talked about working out what you need to do to get there. We will expand on that and work out the three things you want to learn to help you achieve your goal. Schedule them. Could you put them in your diary? Commit to taking the time to do it. Be quarterly focused so that at the end of three months, you've achieved a small step towards your significant life change. Pick something achievable at this time. For example, if you want to be a concert pianist, then you could commit to learning to read music.

Activity 6: Scheduling your Post-it notes

In activities 4 and 5, you got the ideas out. Activity 4 was a brainstorm to work out all of the tasks you need to do to achieve your plan. Activity 5 was adding the detail about who is going to do what.

And in activity 6, you are going to start to pull it all together by thinking about the timeframe of each task. Now is the time to go back to each of your Post-it notes and add some detail about how long each task will take.

Once you have allocated timeframes, you are set for another go at sorting them. Find yourself a great open space – a whiteboard or an office wall – and start sorting the Post-its into logical steps from start to finish.

With a bit of creativity, you can sort them in such a way that they become the start of a basic project plan. Importantly, this process now gives you a step-by-step overview of how you are going to implement your change.

CHAOS AND THE FEMININE

No matter how good you are at planning, life will happen. Plan for this, expect this, and breathe.

You are deluding yourself if you think that project management or planning is the answer to your leadership pain. I can say that because I am a project manager. You are also deluding yourself if you believe that leadership is all about core logic, plans and control. Planning is part of the solution. Planning and order helps, but you will miss out on all the good stuff if you are too rigid and too reliant on your logic, rules and authority.

Better projects happen when creativity, change and innovation are encouraged. Generally, the best teams, projects and businesses are all built in the middle of chaos – not inside a tight structure. And, in my experience, the best project managers, and leaders, are those who lean into the chaos and confusion. Because that is where the gold is; the opportunities for innovation and growth. For everyone.

Start-Up Sandy

I introduced my friend Sandy back in the introduction and principle 1. Sandy and I worked together for many years, and then she set up her own consulting business. Her approach to business was freeform and wild – go with the flow and see what happens. Policies, procedures and systems were not her natural state. I was the project manager with control, logic, systems and management processes in place.

Sandy set her business up in the year before she died. It was a complete mess and thriving – it shouldn't have worked, but it did because she was relationship-oriented. Sandy introduced me to the notion that chaos can be good for change because it helps us respond rather than focusing on what we want to happen.

Your concern might be that people will judge you poorly if they think your project is off the rails. A good change-management process or project-review process will help. A flexible attitude that says, 'Yes, we can adapt as the project matures and our understanding deepens' will also help you to respond to change.

Again, this book is not about project-management techniques or psychological advice. Based on my experience, I have found that better projects and teams happen when you allow for and encourage a bit of messiness.

Activity 7: **Project chaos**

In project management and life, there is nothing more probable than change and chaos. Despite your best efforts, when you start on a project, there is no way possible that you can identify all of the things that might, and will, go wrong.

When working with your team on anything, you need to encourage change management and the learning process. A process to manage change is critical to any business or organisation because it is how you remain proactive, not reactive to the things that happen.

When you come together for a team meeting, you might add to your agenda an item on problems and 'stuff we learned'. Encourage people to talk about the things that have gone wrong during the week, or something they didn't know and that they had to respond to – and encourage a learning culture. You might also have a 'what we could have done better' item on that agenda – how we will do better, and what we learned. Encourage people to talk about the learning journey and the creativity required to adjust rather than focusing on the narrative about what went wrong and how it deviated from what was planned.

Armed with information about the things that have changed, you can then go back to your Post-it notes (and your plan) and make any necessary adjustments. If you find that there have been delays on a task, you can move the schedule around accordingly. If you find that a person can't commit to a task, you can re-assign that task to someone else.

The critical bit is that there will always be change, and with a Post-it note-based plan, you can work with your team to make changes and keep up-to-date.

Production meetings

At our earthmoving business, we manage a team of around ten people across around 30 jobs on a waitlist. Soon after we purchased the company, I asked the team about the forward work schedule and our monthly forecast. I was told in no uncertain terms that 'earthmoving is different' because 'things change all the time'. The more I pushed, the deeper the team dug. There was no way they were going to be organised by a project manager.

Soon after, I tried another technique. We started hosting weekly production meetings to understand what was changing, week to week. And, guess what? Every job was assigned to a Post-it note and then assigned to a column on a whiteboard. The columns were headed up with timeframes. Project management by stealth!

The interesting thing was that once our people got used to the idea of recording jobs and then moving them around according to things that were changing, they began to embrace the concept of project management.

As a leader, you may feel a little uncomfortable with chaos and change. Embrace it, because you set the tone for your team. If you seem to be encouraging a little messiness and a little confusion in the spirit of improvement, then your team will get comfortable with it, too.

CONCLUSION

Projects and life work best when you let your guard down and allow your heart, rather than your head, to take control. Chaos and mess bring about change, innovation and fun. Projects need power, order and boundaries. But the best projects are those that actively seek out innovation and change as a normal part of business.

As a leader, you don't need to be perfect. Chaos happens every day and should be encouraged and embraced. Let go.

Use the techniques that we've talked about in this chapter and map out your plan of attack. Build some tolerance into your schedule for life and chaos. Be ready for it.

Armed with the knowledge that life is part chaos and part order, you are now ready to tackle the next stage. Shit is about to get real. In the next chapter, we will go deeper, get real and own our shit. The honesty required is terrifying, but it's where we need to go if we're going to live out our most profound leadership truths.

3

Take responsibility for your own shit

As I mentioned in the introduction, many of us leaders have adopted the leadership strategies and styles of the people who came before us. These are the leaders who led us, and we modelled their leadership styles. Consciously or not, you will have adopted at least some of the characteristics of your former leaders. It's what everyone does.

Now sometimes, the strategies you've adopted might not feel right to you. You might also notice that the leadership style you've adopted is not getting the results you want.

When you begin to notice that things don't feel comfortable, stop and reflect. Are you being asked to think deeper about your truth, what you truly want out of life? Maybe it is now that you begin to create the leadership style you wish to embody consciously?

This is your chance to become the leader you want to be.

This chapter discusses the exciting change that happens when you become aware of your leadership style and its limitations.

The problem is never about them (them being your people – your team). The problem is about how you, and I mean *you*, perceive the situation. Once you understand that it (the problem) is all about how you perceive it, it becomes a game-changer for your life as a leader. And, when you move towards your life as a heartfelt leader, you'll understand that your intuition is just as important as your logic. Your transition to a heartfelt leader also involves moving from a command-and-control model to a leadership model that is real, human and creates lasting change.

The whole point of this principle is that the only person you can change is you. You must be clear that you have power over how you perceive a situation. You can't, unfortunately, force other people to change. Thinking that you can will only lead to your frustration and stress. Therefore, you need to own your own shit as a starting point.

SANDY AND THE MAIN STREET PUB

My best mate Sandy, whom I've mentioned earlier, gave me some of the most significant learning moments in my journey to becoming a heartfelt leader. About seven years ago, I was a manic project manager who believed in tightly controlling every situation so that it would work out how I wanted it to. At the time, I was teaching leadership – which, on reflection, seems hilarious – to a group of CEOs. I had been called in at the last minute to deliver some training because the booked trainer was sacked that same day.

Although it was at short notice, I was confident I delivered a thought-provoking and insightful session. But, at the end of the session and in the days after, I received feedback from the client that it lacked energy and effort. She was disappointed in me. And, of course, I was enraged that she dared to criticise my session.

Debriefing, I spoke to Sandy at length about this. She took me to a local bar, poured me a large wine and let me rant and rave for quite some time. I expected Sandy to join me on my witch-hunt – take up some pitchforks and go after this client. Fortunately for me, Sandy suddenly turned and said to me, 'So, why has this woman got so far up your arse?' I said, 'Hang on a minute. Wait, what are we talking about?' 'Kerry, you know your stuff, so why are you so upset about her feedback? What's going on for you?'

There was a long pause.

Once I got over the shock of her question, I stopped and thought. Of course, there was a whole bunch of stuff going on for me at the time. My gut knew it, and my heart knew it. They were waiting for my head to catch up.

At that time, I had many personal issues going on – things like a divorce, a tricky personal relationship and little kids adjusting to a new lifestyle. What that meant was I hadn't prepared well for the leadership training and I had delivered a pretty lazy, half-arsed session.

I am forever in debt to Sandy for holding up a mirror to me, myself and I. I specifically credit her for starting me on my heartfelt leadership journey. It was the defining moment where I had to own my own shit and recognise that it was all about me – about what was going on for me, and nothing to do with my client, the participants who had complained or anyone else.

So, as a heartfelt leader, I have learned that to survive and thrive, I need to use my feminine skill set of intuition in tandem with my masculine skill set of logic.

In this chapter, I'll go deeper into the role of intuition, what it means to take responsibility for yourself and your growth, and how to use logic (the stuff between your ears).

INTUITION, AND OWNING YOUR OWN SHIT

Around the middle of your career, you may begin to question whether this is really a life with endless tasks, problems and people to deal with. You might feel like you are constantly reacting to others' issues, and find yourself wondering if this is all there is.

Sandy taught me that the most powerful thing is the importance of owning your shit. This has changed my life ever since. Full stop.

I am talking about taking massive personal responsibility for what happens to you and tapping into this responsibility by listening to your intuition. If you can't hear your intuition yet, have a quiet listen to your gut because that's where your intuition makes the most noise. I'll tell you more about how to do that later in this chapter.

Listening to your intuition will provide you with all the leadership direction you'll ever need. You already have the answers to most of your problems; you just need to listen.

Sandy and my gut

Back at the pub, Sandy reminded me that if I listened to what was going on for myself, I'd find my issue was about something that I needed to deal with rather than tackling my client. The truth is, I already knew what was wrong in my gut. I had a relationship issue going on at the time, and I already knew that I had failed to prepare enough for the session. I was kind of hoping to get away with it. I wanted to blame the client and label her feedback wrong rather than accepting responsibility for my lack of performance. My gut knew that I was the cause, but my brain, my logic, wanted to make it all about her.

You might think that you're not intuitive at all and that this all seems a bit fluffy. You might also believe that you don't know the answer to whatever problem you're facing. But, if you listen very carefully, you'll hear that voice inside your head. It's talking to you all day long, assessing what's happening around you and giving you commentary. Take a quiet moment and listen to what's underneath and what's happening for yourself. Ask yourself the critical question – 'If I did know what to do, what would it be?'

If you did know

I was working with a client, a CEO who disagreed with an enormous decision at work that would impact people's lives. She said, 'I just don't know what to do.' I challenged her. 'If you did know what to do, what would it be?' 'Well, if I did know, and I knew what was about to happen, I would have quit my job.' And she did.

Not for a minute am I suggesting that you rely *only* on your intuition to make decisions. It's a critical source of information that we often disregard when we let our logic and evidence brain take over. Your intuition is one source of information that you should consider, together with the facts.

Activity 8: Accessing your intuition

Daily, start practising accessing your intuition. Get away somewhere quiet. I also like to go for a walk in nature for this one because it means I won't be distracted by phones or people. Take a deep breath, engage your diaphragm and tune into your gut when you are in that quiet space. Feel what your stomach's feeling, feel what your gut is telling you and then ask yourself the question you're pondering.

You will have a whole bunch of feelings and judgements that come with that. Your logical brain will say, 'That can't be right. That's not the case. That's not what's happening.' Access what I call your leadership voice and ask yourself, 'What would a grown-up me do here?' Let the thoughts come and go, and then just sit with that answer. Breathe that answer again; keep focusing on your tummy as you breathe deeply. Then when you've settled on the solution, write the answer down in a journal or on a scrap piece of paper, the back of an envelope, anywhere. You are taking the unconscious thinking and making it conscious, making it real, by putting pen to paper. You don't have to do anything with it, but you've made it real. You've accessed your intuition. You're using this system to get in touch with your intuitive decision-making.

You might be caught in the busyness trap. A busy schedule. A big to-do list. Too much to do and not enough time. But you must make time for quiet reflection. Your reflection might only be 15 or 30 minutes a day, but it's that time away from the phone, the email and the office that allows you to consider what is going on for you.

You might like to schedule a break in your diary every day. It might be before you go to work or at the end of the day once you've knocked off. But the best way to do it is to have a little organisation to your day and find your 15, 20 or 30 minutes.

INTUITION AND THE PARADOX OF GROWTH

As a heartfelt leader, you will learn that tapping into your intuition will help you solve problems. But what happens if you get good at solving problems? Once you get good at solving problems, you get more problems, which I call the paradox of growth. We all hope to live in a utopian world where life is free of problems and is easy, but unfortunately, life isn't about living *without* problems; it's about solving problems. Our most remarkable personal growth comes from our most challenging times. The things that we're most proud of are generally those where we've had to sort some shit out – hard stuff, messy stuff, complicated stuff; stuff that's asked us to grow as a person, where we've had to build new skills, or where we've been vulnerable, and we've had to be wrong until we got it.

Challenge is the new normal for a heartfelt leader. It can be tiresome, but growth is the reward for meeting daily challenges.

Fantasy Monday

I have a fantasy Monday. I get up early, I go to the gym and I do a killer workout. I return home to a house of teenagers who prepare themselves a nutritional breakfast and do all their chores without complaint or my asking. I drop the teenagers off to school with all their required gear and a healthy lunchbox, with their homework done, and then I roll on to work. When I get to work, there's a latte waiting for me. My team is up-to-date on their tasks, and they're ready to attack the world with vigour. None of my customers have concerns, and my bank account has miraculously filled up over the weekend. And all of this is because of my purpose-driven contribution to the world!

Does that sound like your Monday, or is your Monday more like my reality – a hats off, tits out kind of a day where I lurch towards some sort of dream that I've got it all together? Have you been sold an idea that life is meant to be easy and you won't have any problems? You are told that if you are just 'enough' – pretty enough, smart enough, fast enough, organised enough – everything will be okay. But here is the shitty paradox:

41

Our real growth comes from solving problems.

You might be thinking, 'What has my intuition got to do with all of this?'

As a heartfelt leader, you can expect a life full of problems. If you approach problems as a link to personal growth and tune into your intuition to help you solve them, then you can achieve the life of your dreams.

Activity 9: Reframe your problems (before you solve them)

When you are faced with a big problem – maybe something like a problematic staff member – before you tackle it, set up a reframe of the problem with a couple of important questions:

- What is this situation teaching me?

- What can I learn from this situation?

- How will this situation help me grow as a person or a leader?

    Using the example, this translates to:

- What is this situation with this difficult staff member teaching me?

- What can I learn from this staff member or the difficult decision that I'm about to make?

- How will this situation with the staff member, or the decision I need to make, help me to grow as a person and as a leader?

The tantrum

I always tend to say yes, and I take on more than I can generally achieve. In principle 1, I talked about taking on a big project inside our business – a complete rewrite of our work health and safety policies. I spent most of my spare time working on those policies. Sundays and after-hour slogs dragged on for what seemed like forever. I didn't have the time for it, and I hated and resented every single minute of it. On one Sunday, I chucked the biggest tantrum. I was struggling with a pretty tedious policy when I had had enough. I got into my car and drove away from the office because I couldn't stand it any longer. My escape didn't last very long when I found myself 20km from home with no money, phone or idea of where I was going.

When I did the reframe, I asked myself, 'What is this situation teaching me?' I discovered that I needed to learn how to say no. I learned from that situation that my role had changed from being a doer to a leader. Instead of saying yes to *everything*, this situation helped me grow by learning how to set my boundaries as a leader. When I asked myself, 'What can I learn from this situation?' I reflected that rather than being personally responsible for writing those policies, I needed to clarify what I could and couldn't possibly do in my ever-expanding portfolio of work. And, finally, when I asked, 'How has this situation helped me to grow?' I found that it was, in fact, very rich in learning for me. That situation helped me to restructure how I was going to go about this particular business.

Activity 10: **Get yourself back on track**

You might still want to make your problem somebody else's fault. But, here is the thing: you are giving up all of your power when you want to make it somebody else's fault. I know I did. Somehow it was my husband's fault because I said, 'Yes, I will rewrite all of our policies.'

If you find yourself here, go back and repeat the breathing exercise. Remember the heartfelt breathing in activity 1? The breathing that expands your back and shoulders and exhales through your heart?

Go somewhere quiet, get your breathing going, focus on your heart and access the highest version of yourself.

Ask the question, 'What do I need to do here? What's the situation teaching me? What can I learn? And how will this situation help me to grow?'

LOGIC AND THE STUFF BETWEEN YOUR EARS

As a heartfelt leader, it is crucial that you learn to balance your logic and your intuition. I have been working in real estate for the last five years, and before that, I worked in consulting for 20 years. And, in these businesses, I have had many opportunities to see how our perceptions impact our results every day. Interestingly, the situation will almost always play out exactly how we think it's going to.

The homeowner reaction

Let's take the example of a problematic homeowner. If you walk into the meeting with the view that she's going to be difficult and will not sell at that price, it's likely she's going to be difficult. But if you walk into the same meeting with a more curious approach, you are more likely to find a better outcome – maybe not the sale, but some way to help and support the homeowner.

This is the magic crossover point between your intuition and your logic. Your intuition may have told you that the homeowner is likely to be difficult, but your logic will help you systematically approach the situation.

Intuition will help you to craft the question, and logic will allow you to test the answer. Intuition will also help you tune into the homeowner's emotional state, and logic will help you balance the decision with facts, figures and evidence.

Intuition is a critical skill that you need to develop to improve your leadership. Equally, you need to test your assumptions and beliefs with a reality check using your logic.

The 24-hour media cycle, together with our social media consumption patterns, means that we receive so much information that we simply regurgitate the populist opinion, whether we have any evidence or not.

The market is between our ears

I often say in real estate that the market exists between our ears – it's not based on fact or reality; it is simply what we think (or rather feel) about the market. Australia's reaction to real estate during the Covid era gives you the perfect illustration. Price rises of around 20 per cent in 12 months was previously unheard of, and yet, there are still more buyers than sellers pushing up prices in their rush to find their 'new normal'. Despite the evidence, emotional, illogical buyers are keen to throw more money at housing to secure it.

Take a step back from emotionally charged imagery, quotes and the wide variety of talking heads that swim around in our digital world. You can then ask yourself, 'Is this real?' Before you write off the vendor or blame the market for being flat (or high), you need to consider the truth of your reality. What you think, you believe, and that becomes your reality.

Head, heart and gut

You might be a bit confused and unsure whether I want you to be logical or intuitive. I am hoping that you can use both skill sets and a balanced approach when you're making decisions.

Recently, I was fortunate to work with some young and upcoming leaders. The young women in this sports-based team were facing a crisis of confidence about their ability to play as a team and win. They certainly had the technical skills but were letting their opponents' opinions rattle them. I led them through a team leadership process that asked them to temporarily divorce their heads from their hearts and guts.

You might know this feeling, too. When you are scared, where do you feel it first? Likely in the gut. Anxiety and stress often make themselves known first when those butterflies (or worse) appear. Your brain then gets the message that there is something to be scared of, and it gets busy looking for evidence. Armed with proof that the opposition team was, in fact, taller, stronger and faster, these young ladies then collapsed under perceived pressure and went on a long losing streak.

Our great reset was in the retelling of the story of Katniss Everdeen, the heroine of *The Hunger Games*. In the four-part series, Katniss defies life-threatening odds and overcomes her fear (of dying) and becomes her people's hero. My question to the girls was simple: where did Katniss get her courage from? Her head? No – it was full of logic. Her gut? No – it was terrified. Her heart? A resounding yes. And I hope that is true for you, too. You feel your courage in your heart, not your head or your gut.

So while I want you to tune into your gut and your intuition as your source of 'knowing', I don't want you to stay there. Your intuition is an early warning device about what is about to happen. You need your intuition to counter your logic and make good decisions.

Conversely, your head aims to keep you safe and works hard to find evidence that you are in immediate danger. You also need your logic to make rational, evidenced decisions.

But for truly courageous decisions, it is your heart that does the lion's work.

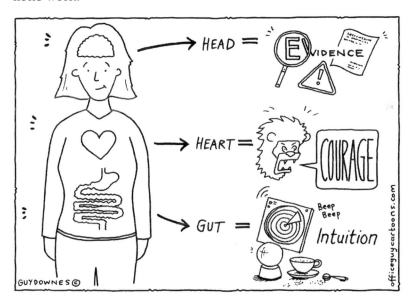

Activity 11: Aligning your head, your gut and your heart

Before making any significant decision or attending an important meeting, find 15 minutes to go back to the breathing exercise to enable you to access your highest and best version of yourself, ask that version of yourself the key questions, and settle on the best response. Once you've got that intuitive response, please test it out with logic. Does the evidence stack up that it's a reasonable decision to make?

You might be about to buy a new house. Ask yourself:

- Is this real? Do I need a new house?

- What am I telling myself here? What story am I telling myself about life in a new house?

- What is the evidence? Where is the market evidence? Where is the family evidence?

- What does my gut tell me? What do I know deep down to be the truth of my decision?

- And, most importantly, what is my heart telling me? What is the courageous decision?

CONCLUSION

A heartfelt leader will access their authentic leadership voice by tapping into their intuition, often found in those feelings in the gut. Tapping into your intuition will give you access to the highest and best version of yourself. Testing your assumptions with logic will also then strengthen your case with your team.

At the highest level, you will need to trust yourself to follow your intuition on those matters.

Access your intuition by getting quiet and asking yourself the critical question, 'If I did know what to do, what would it be?'

Test the truth of your intuition further by breathing into your heart, and ask yourself the question again. 'If I did know what to do, what would it be?'

You are now tuned in and armed with the highest and best version of yourself.

Intuition (gut) + logic (head) + courage (heart) will ensure that you are able to lead from a place of personal authority.

And with this new personal authority you are ready for some conversational combat with the outside world. In the next chapter, we'll be talking about actual conversations with real people.

Have difficult conversations

As a leader in the modern world, you might notice that the leadership style you have adopted is not getting the results you want. You might also find yourself struggling with how to get your team to do stuff and still like you. In this chapter, I will talk about the digital age, where you have almost unlimited access to tools that claim to make your communication easier. You might wonder why it's so hard to communicate with your team, get on with the job and get a straight answer when you have so many tools. If you are busy – aren't we all? – it's so much easier to flick a quick text or an email to speed up the communication process. But in this chapter, I'm going to show you that this probably isn't easier in the long-term because the communication slows down or gets misconstrued, no matter how good your intentions were when you sent the text or the email.

Your relationship with your team members will improve, and things will get done if you consciously choose to communicate well with them. The only thing that really matters is the conversation.

CAR PARK CONVERSATIONS

As a long-term management consultant of more than 20 years, I've been called into lots of organisations to undertake reviews of their problems. A not-for-profit client in the community sector asked me to do an organisational assessment. While I was collecting the evidence about how the organisation was performing strategically, I noticed a communication trend.

All roads led to the relationship between the board and the CEO. While the relationship was polite and respectful, it wasn't effective. The chair would moan about the CEO's lack of activity on specific projects. In turn, the CEO would moan about the chair's lack of leadership at a board level. And the board members were caught up in this stand-off, not sure how to change it. When I was finally tired of the chair complaining about the latest board meeting and the CEO's lack of attention, I said to him – and this is a very clever consulting term – 'You guys need to have a car park conversation.'

In my world, a car park conversation takes place off-site, and generally in private. You have a car park conversation to clear the air and to provide direct and meaningful feedback.

In this situation, both parties were being polite at work, and they lacked the courage to call out each other's behaviour. So tackling the chair first, I outlined how to go about a car park conversation. I explained, 'Please keep it simple, keep it direct and keep it kind, but by all means, HAVE THE CONVERSATION!'

To everyone's surprise, the chair took this on board and had the conversation, literally in the car park after the next board meeting. It started a revolution – but more about that later.

Activity 12: Car park conversations

Having a real-time face-to-face conversation is all that really matters.

A heartfelt leader knows that, as far as relationships go, we've never been so connected digitally and yet so far apart in our understanding. To get traction with your people, you need to be in the same arena, in the same trenches or on the same bus. This can only happen if you're brave enough to have that conversation. A conversation that feels difficult and uncomfortable will do more to help correct a project or business course than silence or a digital message ever could.

Because conversations that matter build the best of relationships.

RELATIONSHIPS – WE HAVE NEVER BEEN SO CONNECTED AND YET SO FAR APART

Covid-19 has changed our lives. Many of us have found that we can work anywhere and at any time. While this is fabulous and makes us more productive, responsive and connected, our relationships at work are less connected than before. Projects are slowing down and misunderstandings are rising. We've lost the art of conversation and simple, old-fashioned human contact. A quick text, an email at midnight or a snipe on a colleague's document doesn't hurt the sender, but it certainly doesn't help the receiver.

It is pretty simple. Your job as a heartfelt leader is to connect people.

Email warfare

As a project manager and consultant, I've witnessed the crucifixion of good people in an awful trial by email.

I am sure you know the emails that I'm talking about. It could be the follow-up email that pops up after a face-to-face or Zoom meeting that starts pretty innocently. Kerry sends it because she didn't like Bob's point in the meeting and feels she needs to correct him by email with evidence that she was right and he was wrong.

But. She not only sends the email to the offender (Bob) but to the whole team. And Bob certainly can't ignore the tone of the email. So Bob decides to respond with his version of why he was right and Kerry was wrong. Of course, the whole team gets copied in on his response. Before too long, Kerry and Bob have a two-way email contest going on to prove who's right and who's wrong, with the whole team watching as interested bystanders in the email ping-pong of the century.

ANOTHER EMAIL SINKS TO THE BOTTOM OF THE INBOX...

This is an example of how quickly emails can escalate a minor misunderstanding.

Conversely, you can get a situation where the email sits there, and nothing happens.

Activity 13: Have the conversation and THEN send the email

The most common excuse that I hear from clients for emailing rather than connecting face-to-face is, 'If I put my request in email, there'll be a record of what was said and what I asked.'

I want to challenge that and say, 'Let's use email to confirm what happened in your conversation.' Again, let's have a conversation with the other person. And then you can use email to confirm what was agreed. Your email could say something like, 'Thanks for the chat. Here's what we've agreed to.' There is then no need to try to negotiate via email.

When you're having a face-to-face conversation, take the time to think about what you want to say and revisit the deep breathing activities that we talked about in principle 3. Access the best version of yourself, and then say it rather than writing it.

Having a real-time conversation with somebody face-to-face takes more courage than it does to send an email. Do it anyway. Because every time you try and you practise it, you'll get better at it. Remember: if it goes wrong, it's a learning opportunity.

RELATIONSHIPS AND THE ARENA

Our modern workplaces can be a lot like the Roman Colosseum. At the Colosseum, a small number of people slug it out to the death for the entertainment of others. At work, we tend to have a large audience of voyeurs whom the leader is also entertaining. Voyeurs, and the crowd, pass judgement on the relative skill or decision of the leader. And with 'no skin in the game', it is easy for the crowd to pass comment on what they 'would have done'.

Or, as Theodore Roosevelt, the 26th American President, put it so much more eloquently:

> *It is not the critic who counts; not the man who points out how the strong man stumbles, or where the doer of deeds could have done them better. The credit belongs to the man who is actually in the arena, whose face is marred by dust and sweat and blood; who strives valiantly; who errs, who comes short again and again, because there is no effort without error and shortcoming; but who does actually strive to do the deeds; who knows great enthusiasms, the great devotions; who spends himself in a worthy cause; who at the best knows in the end the triumph of high achievement, and who at the worst, if he fails, at least fails while daring greatly, so that his place shall never be with those cold and timid souls who neither know victory nor defeat.*

My point being, the arena (or the Colosseum) is where heartfelt leaders hang out. They are bloody, muddy and bruised because of their efforts to make a difference and keep making a difference.

Roosevelt prewarns us with his observation that led to his timeless quote:

*The poorest way to face life is to face it with a sneer. A cynical
habit of thought and speech, a readiness to criticize work
which the critic himself never tries to perform, an intellectual
aloofness which will not accept contact with life's realities – all
these are marks, not ... of superiority but weakness.*

Nothing binds us together better than having a shared history
and a story about that time we did something. This is invaluable in
building long-term team culture.

Relationships grow when we have a shared story about over-
coming a hardship together.

Vulnerability and netball

Over the last couple of years, I've been fortunate to lead a local
community sporting organisation. Challenged by population and
distance, our club is a small one. To bring about some overdue
change, I proposed to change the association bylaws. This was
met with resistance from the outside over and over, but that's a
whole other story. I represented the club at a high-level meeting at
a critical juncture, and it didn't go well. It was awful. But what did
go well was me sharing the war story with the girls back at the club,
including the part where I cried in the car on the way home for an
hour. That created a mutual enemy, which did more to strengthen
our club culture than any team building could ever do.

I allowed myself to be vulnerable in front of my club members,
told them the story, and told them how wrong it had gone.

Two things surprised me. In the first instance, my vulnerability
helped to build our internal culture. And, secondly, it created a
common goal to bring about change.

To sum it up, it takes great courage to lead change and challenge the status quo or put our hands up to volunteer outside our comfort zone.

You might not want to show that you're vulnerable or weak in front of your team. However, I've found that showing your vulnerability genuinely and humanly will do more to encourage your team to buy in on an issue than any team building or culture-creating session can.

Activity 14: Things that keep me awake at night

So, how to make this real in your workplace? Try adding an agenda item to your next team meeting titled 'Things That Are Keeping Me Awake at Night' and ask your team members to share what is concerning them. You should go first and share, openly, what is keeping you awake and then invite your team to do the same.

You might have been taught that leaders should be strong and have all the answers. But in the modern workplace, your team is looking for genuine connection, and taking the first step by sharing your true feelings about an issue is significant. I'm sure you will see your relationships change and improve.

Take small steps and build up the trust gradually. I don't encourage anybody to drop their metaphorical pants on day one. Instead, I encourage you to share your concerns about a project or your worries about a budget and allow people to see that you are human and don't have all the answers. As that trust grows, you might share more of your feelings.

RELATIONSHIPS AND CANDID CONVERSATIONS

It takes courage to both build a relationship and to maintain it. The art of conversation, particularly candid conversation, is being lost within our digital age.

Your job as a heartfelt leader is to support your team to grow and develop. Your relationships will prosper when you have shared challenges and candid conversations.

Your team members want to know how they're doing and how they can improve. Your job as a heartfelt leader is to give them this gift.

Radical candour

In her book *Radical Candor*, Kim Scott talks about a time when she was given direct feedback by her boss, Sheryl Sandberg, who was CEO of Facebook. Kim shares that it changed her life because

Sheryl was both empathetic and direct. Sheryl gave Kim specific feedback for improvement couched in natural warmth.

Many of the coaching clients I've worked with have never received constructive – or any – feedback from their line manager. And some of those clients are in their 40s! Imagine spending 20 years in the workforce and never receiving any feedback from your manager!

Activity 15: Plan for and deliver constructive feedback

You might be asking, 'What if I offend my team members by giving them constructive feedback?' The way you approach feedback is critical. If your feedback is given with good intentions to help this person grow their skills, it will lead to learning on both sides.

But first! Get clear about what you want to share with the other person. For example, 'I need to give this person feedback on their writing style.' Make sure that your intentions are good. Is this feedback really about helping to improve this person's writing?

And, secondly, before you deliver the feedback, find your quiet place, check in with your belly and ensure that you're accessing the highest and best version of yourself. Make sure that your feedback is genuinely focused on the other person's growth and learning. Ask yourself, will this feedback help them?

I also like to ask permission. This can be as simple as, 'Are you open to feedback about your project or your writing, and how might you improve?'

If the person says, 'Yes,' they're already indicating that they're receptive to receiving feedback. Then frame your input about the tangible – what needs to be improved, their contribution and how they can progress. Be kind but direct. This will be uncomfortable for you at first.

Ask them to reiterate the feedback that they've heard. This is important. 'Can you summarise what you've heard me say?' Then they can sort that out in their heads, and you can check that your message has been received as intended.

Direct feedback

In my career I have employed a lot of people. Recently I was lucky enough to work with a new creative type who was going to assist my business to move forward. As these new relationships start, everything was good, sweet even. It was the honeymoon period. But, over time, I noticed that there was a mismatch in our understanding. As early as possible, I set up a meeting and asked at the beginning of it, 'Could we have a direct conversation?' With an okay from the other person I outlined with some candour some base misunderstandings. This was a very difficult conversation for me because I knew in my heart that it wasn't working. Over the next few weeks we had another couple of conversations. Each time I sought to be more direct and clear about my expectations. Unfortunately, not long after, that person chose to move on to other things. And while this isn't the perfect story, it does demonstrate that as heartfelt leaders we need to listen to our heart and gut and then have the important conversation.

You might feel uncomfortable and be concerned that they won't like you if you give them constructive feedback. Again, check in that your intentions are good and make sure that you're not just telling them off – that you are there for their growth and their development. If you are happy that your feedback is genuine, then have the courage to step into your leadership role. Our number-one role as humans, and leaders, is to grow and evolve; we do no service to others or ourselves if we avoid these conversations.

DIFFICULT CONVERSATIONS LEAD TO BETTER RESULTS

Australians, by nature, are very polite. Despite their dry sense of humour in the workplace, most of my clients would rather avoid a difficult conversation and hope that things get better by being patient and giving it time. However, a difficult conversation will short-circuit the pain of misunderstanding, poorly planned projects and missed targets. A difficult conversation will also get you to the end game faster. It's like pulling a Band-aid off. Things get better or are completed when a heartfelt leader cares enough about a team or a person to spend the time and energy required to have a difficult conversation.

Avoiding difficult conversations is disrespectful to the people you lead because you're not putting the work in to support their growth.

Funding feedback

I'm a project manager by trade, born and bred. In my early days, I thought that project management meant that I needed to be in control and always right. I also thought that a project plan was a rule book and that no deviations were allowed. In reality, and with maturity, I've learned that the best projects come wrapped around challenges.

Once, when I was working with my project team on a major funding bid, we worked like dogs to meet a deadline – only to have our bid declined. It meant that we had to apply for a second time. After round two, we missed out again. It was only after around three that we saw the holes in our arguments and the gaps in our knowledge. In round three, we were finally successful in a major multi-million-dollar bid.

After each round, we had to have a difficult conversation with the funding partner and then with each other to identify where the gaps were and what we were doing wrong. If we hadn't had those conversations, we wouldn't have achieved the deal.

The most common avoidance reason that I hear across all my coaching clients is, 'I don't like conflict.' A difficult conversation is not a model to manage conflict. A difficult conversation does not need to finish with a right or wrong outcome. It is simply feedback that the receiving party can choose to respond to however they like.

A difficult conversation is, therefore, a growth tool.

Activity 16: Candid conversations

If you are keen, there are loads of ways to avoid a difficult conversation.
   You can:

- get way too busy

- reschedule often

- ask somebody else to do it

- try to have a difficult conversation by text or email

- or, simply forget.

Does any of the above sound familiar to you?

If so, take yourself back up to activity 15 and start to prepare yourself for a candid conversation.

Then prepare an informal agenda for yourself to reflect on before the conversation. This could include:

- Focus on what is going well, both with the situation and the person

- Keep to the facts

- Assume that the other person is working to the best of their ability

- Get to the point quickly

- Be kind, but direct

- Say it and wait for a response

- Avoid filling in the blanks with talking.

You might find yourself lacking confidence in your own opinion and doubting yourself. If this happens, you can check in with your gut and check your evidence. Seek counsel from a trusted source. And then do it anyway.

CONCLUSION

The most profound and most successful relationships and teams are created through mutual respect. And all that really matters is having the courage to HAVE THE CONVERSATION.

Respect is built in the trenches by doing tough stuff together and calling each other's bullshit.

You will need to build a high level of courage – courage that comes from the heart – that you are doing the right thing, for this human and their growth.

Invest in your relationships by taking the time to talk to your team or the individual. Rather than sending a quick email or a text to correct a behaviour, seek out your team member and have a conversation.

Real leaders have real conversations about things that matter.

In the next chapter, the magic happens. Let's talk about how you can lead your team to punch above their weight and kick some big, hairy, audacious goals together.

5

Choose your words

This principle is all about your role as a leader. You might have drifted into the role because you're good at the stuff you do – this is the case for many leaders. You know the technical things like how to be a good nurse, how to be good at property, how to be good at customer service, and suddenly you find yourself in a leadership role because you're good at fixing stuff.

Then you inherit a team of good people who sometimes do dumb shit – or at least that's what you might be secretly thinking. They come to you with problems, and guess what tends to happen? You fix them. And then, as a reward for fixing problems? You get more problems, more people and more stuff to fix. If you've ever wondered how to get people to do stuff so that you don't have to do it, then this is the chapter for you.

If you, as a leader, want to have more time for thinking and more time for strategy, you need to learn how to get people to do the things you want them to. Otherwise, you're going to end up doing it all yourself.

As a leader, the words that you use matter a lot. In this chapter, I will show you the difference between successful words and stuck words, which help you get more things done with your people.

THE ROYAL SHOW

In every leadership role that I've been in, I've been guilty of being the person who fixes stuff. Often it was easier than taking the time to teach and show others how to do it. This might sound familiar to you. In my late 20s, I was a project manager, and I organised a significant event at the Royal Show. I was a very poor leader. I thrived working by the 'it's quicker to do this myself' model of leadership.

We had a ginormous bump in – the event industry term for setting up an event – and I had a team of about 20 people that I was organising, but I couldn't delegate to save myself. The result was that, on the opening day of the Royal Show, I sat down on a box in the store and cried my heart out. This was the start of a major flu that morphed into a chest infection and nearly three weeks away from work. I'd fallen into the trap that when people presented me with problems, I went about fixing them rather than involving them in the solution.

This chapter is about the language that you use as a leader and mastering that language. We're going to look at using your heartfelt leadership skill set of using both feminine (caring) skills and masculine (tough) skills to elicit a better response from your team through language. I am then going to talk about the difference between success language and stuck language.

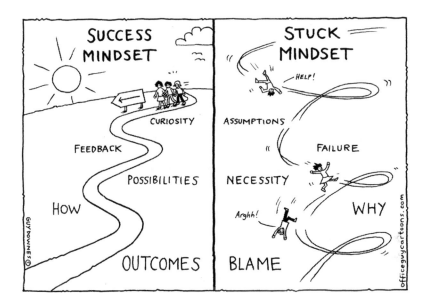

OUTCOMES VERSUS BLAME

As a heartfelt leader, you want to help people, but you also want to help them learn. You want to help people get stuff done – but, most importantly, the right stuff. You may often find yourself stuck in the blame game, trying to decipher who's right and wrong. The quickest way to escalate a situation, any situation, is through your language.

When you're under pressure, you might find yourself asking questions like, 'What's wrong?' and 'Who's to blame?' The quickest way to de-escalate and solve problems with your team is to ask better questions. In this topic, I'm going to show you how three success questions can save the day.

As leaders, we can easily fall into the witch-hunt trap and look for whose fault it is. Often we do that by accident because we are conditioned with questions that we use automatically. Spend time looking at solutions and what outcomes you want to help yourself stay on track. Think again back to principle 1 and get clear about what you want.

Covid-19 impact

When Covid-19 hit in March of 2020, my holiday real estate business lost $300,000 of revenue overnight through lost and cancelled bookings. It would have been easy for us as a team, or for me as a leader, to say, 'Whose fault is this? Who's to blame?' and look to apportion fault and blame somebody else. Instead, as a team, we sat down and asked ourselves three key success questions, which resulted in us turning the business around in 12 months. Of course, we also took a whole lot of action on a bunch of stuff. We rebuilt websites and put a customer relationship management system in place. We also revamped some of our other business systems and cleaned up our marketing, but we did all of those things after asking ourselves the three core questions.

You might be thinking, 'What if I don't find out who or what caused the problem? I might not be able to fix it if I don't understand what created the situation.' Using language and conscious questions will help you engage your team and get more people involved in the problem-solving process, rather than having to do it on your own.

Activity 17: Outcomes versus blame

When a problem blows up, take a breath and then ask yourself these three magical questions, just like my team did when we were at ground zero:

1. Where are we now?

2. Where do we need to be?

3. What is the gap?

Once we'd answered those three questions, we followed them up with two more:

1. What resources do we need?

2. What actions do we need to take?

Instantly, that gave us a plan of attack to resolve and find our way forward.

Because of the way that you've learned about leadership and believed that leaders have all the answers, you might feel like you're not doing your true leader's job when you involve your team in the problem-solving. But fixing stuff keeps you from strategically focusing on your real job, which is to help everyone, including yourself, grow. This is a shift from the masculine taking charge and fixing role to the feminine nurturing and growth role.

HOW VERSUS WHY

As leaders, we spend the best part of our day communicating. I believe that you can always find a better way to communicate. The best measure of how successfully you're communicating is how on board your team is. I'm going to share my single favourite switch and my single favourite hack in this section. Try these at home with your teenagers, and you'll never look back.

The number-one job of a heartfelt leader is to bring about change by enlisting other people's support. You're more likely to do this if you shift your language, and in doing so, move your team's focus from why something happened to how you're going to fix it. When you do that, it will completely change the energy in the room.

The dishes

At home, I have three children ranging in age from 16 to 21. Nothing grinds my gears more than when I come home from work after a long day to a sink full of dishes. I'm confident that you know this feeling. 'Why didn't the dishes get done?' The response is pretty typical – a bunch of excuses. 'It was Charli's turn.' 'It was Chelsea's turn.' 'I didn't have time.' 'I didn't know that it was my job.'

When you ask the 'why' question, you will notice that you are met with a defense response. Try it out with a simple reframe when you get home tonight. Instead of saying, 'Why didn't the dishes get done?' ask, 'How are we going to eat tonight?' You'll feel the difference.

Tongue in cheek, teenagers are a different animal. It's part of our conditioning right from when we were toddlers to have a deep need to understand. When we're looking to understand, we often start questions with 'why'.

You are likely to get a defense response if you're asking 'why?' all the time. Shift your 'whys' to 'hows' and see what changes. This is a habit that I'm going to encourage you to practise for 21 days.

You can try this even with a partner or a friend. When they come to you with a problem, ask them, 'How can we make this happen?' Feel the difference in the energy. The energy bounces back to them to be part of the solution. Notice when you ask, 'Why did this happen?' the energy will land at your feet. And, notice that this issue then becomes your problem, not theirs.

Activity 18: 'How' versus 'why'

Teenagers are the exception to every rule. Your job as a heartfelt leader is to help your team, including the teenagers. So, let's help them shift their energy from 'why' to 'how' through daily practice. Practise using 'how' versus 'why' every day and in every situation. If you want to get your team on board, start your meeting with the simple question – 'How can we do whatever the task is?'

Some useful questions include:

• How has this problem been maintained?

• How is our current set-up contributing to the problem?

• How can you solve the problem?

Work health and safety resistance

As an example, in my current team, we're implementing a new business-wide work health and safety strategy that, at times, is met with resistance. When I'm working with the blokes on-site, they're giving me resistance and saying things like, 'This is all too much, Kerry, this is too hard.' The best way to overcome this resistance is to not buy into the 'why' but rather 'How can we make this safe?' The transition is amazing. Suddenly they are full of solutions and ideas about how to fix the problem, instead of complaining about it.

Your language habits are going to be the hardest thing to shift here. The words that you use are ingrained in you. Take conscious action to practise, practise, practise. When somebody comes to you with a problem, ask them 'how' rather than 'why'.

POSSIBILITIES VERSUS NECESSITIES

When you're stuck on a problem, you might find that you get focused on what you 'have to do' or the necessity of what is going on rather than what's possible. You might find that you and your team will be asking questions like, 'What do we have to do?', 'What do we want?' and 'When's the deadline?', which gets you focused on necessity.

You give away your power when you focus on necessity. Especially when you say things like, 'The boss wants it by tomorrow' or 'The government wants it that way.'

I will share some other questions that can help you and your team move from a stuck state or stuck language to something lighter and more productive by using success-based language.

When you are under pressure and busy – and who's not busy? – you tend to catastrophise everything: 'I have to do this. I have to get this done.' A heartfelt leader will use both a caring and a tough approach by asking better questions to consider what's possible. I'm going to outline some simple ways to do this.

Redundant financial reports

When I was working as a consultant about ten years ago, I worked with a large organisation trying to improve productivity. One of their sacred cows – the things that were important to them – was the finance team's reports. Producing these reports was taking up a considerable amount of the finance team's working week. Then, as a group, everyone in the organisation had to look at the reports – and there were about 20 of them.

I asked the finance team, 'If you stopped doing those reports, would anybody notice?' Guess what? Nobody even noticed that the reports had stopped coming to them – the team and I replaced them with higher-level, more straightforward performance reports.

Activity 19: Possibility versus necessity

You might feel that you're not empowered to make a decision and that you have to do a particular thing for your boss, your company, your wife or your family. Take a deep breath and, for a minute, consider what's possible.

Of course, there are exceptions to this rule: things like your tax, legal stuff, regulatory stuff and things you must do to continue functioning.

In the middle of a 'have to' moment, walk away from your desk and consider. I like to go outside and feel the grass under my feet. Ask yourself these key questions:

- What is possible in this situation, here and now?
- How can we make this happen?
- What are our other options?

Write the answers down and make it real. We're taking the possibility out of your head and into reality.

The biggest barrier you're going to face is other people saying, 'We have to.' Ask them to put that conversation to one side for a minute and then ask them the same questions you asked yourself.

FEEDBACK AND FAILURE

When you focus on failure and what went wrong, you cannot see the lesson or grow your understanding. Typically, you will find yourself asking questions that will keep you straight, like, 'Why did that fail? What went wrong? Who's to blame?' Again, you are looking for a reason. When you do that, the blame is so big that it's at a 'never coming back' level. If your energy, and your team's energy, is at that 'never coming back' level, it will possibly destroy your team. I am going to suggest different ways to seek out the hidden gold in your problems.

A learning culture gives us longevity rather than a short shelf life with an ending. If you approach things from a learning culture, you will keep growing as a team. If you are doing the opposite, someone's going to get sacked.

The Challenger

In the mid-1980s, the United States government was under pressure to launch a space shuttle and get to the moon. That put a lot of pressure on the engineering team. The space shuttle Challenger launched and, 73 seconds into its flight, exploded and killed all of the seven crew members aboard. Later on, there was an investigation, and the technical reason for the explosion was a tiny O-ring that failed and brought the shuttle down.

When the Reagan government did the investigation, it found that an engineer on the team had been consistently raising this O-ring malfunction. The fault had been dismissed, for many years, because of the culture inside the business. Rather than safety and innovation, the Challenger team culture encouraged fault and blame. When the government finished the investigation, it deemed the O-ring a critical part. And, as a vital part, its function should never have been ignored.

What really happened inside the Challenger team was that the leaders were not asking the critical questions like, 'How do we do this better? What's possible here?' until it was too late.

The disaster resulted in a 32-month break in the space shuttle program and the formation of the Rogers Commission, appointed by the then-President of the United States, Ronald Reagan, to investigate the accident. The Rogers Commission found that NASA's organisational culture and decision-making process were the key contributing factors to the accident.

You might think that you don't have time to debrief or look at the feedback because the pressure's on you to move on to the next project, the next thing, the next crisis. You might also be concerned that, as a leader, feedback might show you that you didn't do your job well. But your fundamental role as a heartfelt leader is to ask questions every day and take responsibility for the answers.

Activity 20: Feedback versus failure

Debrief your experience on a project or an issue in a team meeting before starting the next project or the next cycle. It only needs to take about an hour. Have all responsible team members there – people who worked on the task – but treat it like a celebration. Bring some cake or have some exceptional coffee, and then ask somebody in the room to record the findings.

It can be as simple as some notes on a whiteboard or a piece of butcher's paper. Keep those findings and share them officially in what I would call an organisational learning library. In my team, we have a much simpler model where it's just a folder of stuff we learned saved in a shared Google Drive.

In that debriefing, ask yourself questions as a team, like:

- What's happened so far?

- What have we learned?

- What could we do differently?

- How will we know when that project or that thing is a success?

This is not an activity to go looking for blame, but rather a move to look for what we learned from that process. You are looking for feedback.

Culturally, this may take a lot of time to implement. Your team might think that you're looking to blame someone or for a scapegoat if something went wrong. Through your heartfelt leadership, you can consistently demonstrate that you're looking for learnings through celebrations.

CURIOSITY VERSUS ASSUMPTIONS

As leaders and humans, we tend to jump to conclusions and assumptions about what's happening and what other people think. You can fall into the trap of saying things like, 'You know this,' or 'You think that,' or 'It's obvious that they're going to do this' or 'They are X.' I'm going to show you, again, some better questions to test your assumptions and be more curious about the results.

If you are more curious as a leader, you allow yourself to be more creative about the solution and *make things that matter happen.*

It won't rent at that price!

The real estate world is full of deals, and often agents like me are in a situation where the buyer or the vendor is making assumptions about what the other person's thinking, or the market's making assumptions. A classic example comes from inside my team. We listed a property for rent for what seemed to us an astronomical price at the time. Members of my team were making comments like, 'They won't rent it at that price. Our market's never had a rental at that price.'

I needed to challenge my team about what we were assuming here. We are not the market. Just because *we* might not pay that price for rent doesn't mean others won't. We've got a different value system from others, and other people in the market may not have the same belief system or the same level of values as we do. I suggested that we test the market and see what type of feedback we got. Feedback from the potential tenants was that they thought it was cheap for the location, the amenities and the features of the house that we were offering.

You must get evidence to test your assumptions rather than basing your decision-making around your own belief systems.

You might feel that it's difficult for you to stop assuming things because of your experience. It will take some time and expertise to learn how to check your assumptions. Practise asking better questions.

Activity 21: Curiosity versus assumptions

Ask better questions, such as, 'What are we assuming here?' In the example of the rented property, we're assuming that the market won't pay that price. What are we thinking about them, their thoughts, or their reactions? We're assuming that they've got the same budget, same lifestyle choices, and same approach that we have. What has to be true for this to be a real issue is if the tenants or the renters come back to us and say, 'It's too expensive.'

Some other questions that help here are:

• What are you assuming about their thoughts or reactions?

• What has to be true for this to be a problem?

Often, when you are a technical expert and have been in a job, an industry or a field for a long time, you believe that you already know the answers. As you have seen with Covid-19, things change. It is always worth checking your assumptions with the people around you – both close to you and those outside your sphere of influence.

CONCLUSION

In this chapter, you have learned that simple words can make a huge difference in getting the best out of your team. A simple switch from a stuck word like 'why' to 'how' can uncover new ways of doing the things that you do.

As a heartfelt leader, you will need to consciously swap some of your language so that it's both caring and challenging by ever so gently moving the responsibility for action from you to your team.

Practise your language by swapping from a stuck state or a stuck language to a success state or success language. Focus on the five topics that we've talked about and move from:

- blame to outcomes
- why to how
- necessity to possibilities
- failure to feedback
- assumptions to curiosity.

By reading this chapter, you now have the power to transform your relationship with your team.

Because words matter. When you choose your words you have the power to get more things done. And you now have clever language choices that shift the ownership of problems to your team.

In the next chapter, you will sustain this transformation through solid techniques that will keep you accountable.

6

Keep it real for you and your team

As a leader in early 2020, would you have ever thought that our world would so entirely change due to a global pandemic? And yet, life goes on. Regardless of the change and uncertainty, your business, team and organisation still need to make things happen. On the one hand, you are asked to manage business as usual. On the other hand, you are asked to adapt. How does a heartfelt leader manage this balancing act?

In times like this, a lack of personal and team accountability lets us off the hook. Conversely, a lack of innovation and change also means that we go backward.

As a heartfelt leader, you will deliver results and create change with your team. But, leading change will require equal doses of responsibility and innovation. If you don't get the balance right, your team will either be highly disciplined and get lots of stuff done or in complete chaos and jumping from one idea to the next. You want them to be productive, effective and responsive to change.

ALL CARE AND NO RESPONSIBILITY

In my consulting days, I was working in the not-for-profit space with a service-based organisation. The business was highly feminine in its orientation – it had female leaders, senior female leaders, and, generally, made very emotive decisions. Employees at the organisation naturally developed great relationships, and had excellent levels of client care and incredible levels of innovation. However, they also had insufficient evidence and inadequate business systems to track their relationships and innovation. They had very little accountability for money or resources. The organisation was also bordering on being financially bankrupt and leaders were often worried about how they would pay wages.

I worked with them to introduce some core project-management concepts and accountabilities. Using those fundamental techniques, we were able to turn the business around within a two-year timeframe, to the point where it was trading with a surplus and had business systems that could account for that.

One of the organisation's core strengths was that it was highly in tune with what its clients needed. It was able to respond to changes in the marketplace quickly and adaptively because it understood its clients well. Because of this reputation, it could get the business support it needed to ensure profitability.

In principle 1, you worked out what you want. In principle 2, you planned your attack. In principle 3, you took responsibility for yourself. In principle 4, you had a difficult car park conversation. In principle 5, you polished up your words. This chapter will talk about excellent project management. It will also discuss how a heartfelt leader can find the balance between their masculine skill set and need for responsibility and their feminine skill set and need for innovation.

In this chapter, I will talk about the responsibility you have as a leader in your team, and for meeting your agreements. I will also talk about innovation and how you, as a leader, can actively build change processes into business systems.

RESPONSIBILITY, AND ENSURING YOUR TEAM MEETS ITS AGREEMENTS

I have learned that project management is both an art and a science. The science part is the numbers, the logic, the timeframes, the costs, the schedules and the tasks. These can be worked out, and can be absolute. The art part is the humans, the crisis, the change, the emotions and an organisation's culture. These are a lot more nebulous and harder to identify. As heartfelt leaders, we need to be skilled and adept in both the art and the science of leadership.

As Tony Robbins says, 'Energy goes where attention goes.' If you do not make sure that your team members are doing what they said they would do, you quickly descend into chaos. And, guess what? Not much gets done.

The Royal Show flu crisis

In principle 4, I talked about my inability to delegate to my team when I was in my late 20s and working as a project manager on an exhibition event at the Royal Show. Those were the days when I was in deep project management control. I had everything scheduled, budgeted, timed and controlled. Except two things went wrong – I got very sick, and I did everything myself. I quickly learned the importance of delegating and getting clear with a shared understanding of task management: and who's going to do what, by when.

You might be thinking, 'I'm not a project manager, nor do I have the project-management skills that you keep talking about – I have people skills.' Perfect! Even better! This makes you exactly the right person to manage the situation. Would you please facilitate the conversation to ensure everybody knows what's happening, that it's written down, and that the team understands it?

Activity 22: An accountable team meeting

When you're starting on a new project or a new initiative, bring your team together, particularly the people you critically work with. Hold a team meeting, which might be two or three hours. Make sure you've got food and are in a comfortable room that will not allow people to be distracted. Please turn off the phones and then go back to the questions that we used in principle 5. Ask, 'How will we approach this project, thing or event?' Ask somebody to capture the ideas about what you need to do and how you need to do it by writing them down on Post-it notes.

Use a big wall and pop each Post-it note idea on the wall. Sort the chunks of tasks into groups. Your job in this meeting is to facilitate the conversation. Your job is to ask questions about each of those tasks: 'What's reasonable? What's not?' Facilitate a discussion about the best course of action. The most important thing that you can do in this meeting – and this is learning from the days when I worked with my not-for-profit groups – is that you need to assign a *single name* to a *single task* or *action*.

Lots of us want to work on things together. Kath and Kerry might decide to do the task of organising the office together. What generally happens is that Kath thinks that Kerry's doing it, and Kerry thinks that Kath is doing it. And it doesn't get done. Make sure that a single name goes onto a single note, and that person is responsible for making that thing happen. They might not necessarily do it, but they are the person who is going to be held accountable.

Once you've got names on all those Post-it notes, you can write them up in a task list and circulate that task list for agreement across the team. You can then agree to another meeting at some point in the future – preferably about two weeks – where you can refer back to your task lists and check on where people are. People have then got time to go away, investigate, explore the task, do some work and get the job moving. Having a two-week timeframe between meetings also means if it's wrong or needs to change, there's still time for that to happen.

Activity 23: Your next accountable team meeting

At the meeting two weeks later, you come back with your agreed document and look at how you are tracking against that progress. Of course, most people in the room will be most concerned about those tasks that have their name next to them, because they are human. This is the secret. This human tension will help your team stay accountable for getting the job done.

The beautiful thing about project management is discovering what has changed when you have your follow-up meeting. You identify new tasks to add to the list and delete items that are no longer relevant, are unimportant or are finished.

You might feel like you don't want to tell your managers or your team what to do. But you are a heartfelt facilitator whose job is to ask questions. Use the 'how' technique of asking them – 'How can we make this happen?' – to elicit their involvement in the project.

INNOVATION, AND ACTIVELY BUILDING IN CHANGE

The best projects, people and teams that I've worked with have generally resulted from a tragedy, a disaster or a common enemy. (By tragedy, I mean when things are messy, crazy or scary – like Covid-19 or losing a contract.) In most cases there's been a plan that's gone wrong, or somebody's let the team down. I would say that these, in fact, are the best days of my life. This mess or tragedy is your opportunity to create, innovate and change. Heartfelt leaders build tolerance for change into all of their projects, their people and their teams for precisely this reason. Nobody could have predicted a pandemic would arrive, or that we needed to build that space into our organisations.

In these moments, there's an excellent opportunity for you to regroup, rebuild and work out what you need to innovate and change to respond to that. Innovation and change generally happen in response to something complicated. They don't happen when things are going well, because you are comfortable.

Change is the only thing that's constant in our lives. As a heartfelt leader, you need to expect it, embrace it and plan for it. I have also learned that there is no space for amendment, improvement or change when I am aiming for total control.

A flat-pack shed

When I was newly single in my late 30s, I found myself sitting in a paddock with a flat-pack shed and house where a husband used to be. I had carefully constructed a white-picket-fence lifestyle – two kids, one dog and a husband. What I found was that I had a massive 'sexually transmitted debt' post-divorce. I had no income and two small children. It was not the well-planned existence that I believed that I was going to have.

It was a huge shed. And the shed was intended to be a workshop for my now ex-husband.

I looked at the shed and the paddock.

I looked at my bank balance.

I looked at the shed and the paddock again, and I turned that shed into a bunch of storage units.

I turned that shed into money to pay the mortgage.

I learned that the pressure and reality of a pretty tough situation pushed me to be more innovative. I responded to that challenging situation with some creativity.

Activity 24: Accountability by stealth

Now, you might be thinking that your board, boss or organisation won't let you deviate from the plan you presented to them. The trick is to disguise your suggestions as a risk-management plan. 'Here are some risks that I've identified in our plan. What shall we do about these risks?' People are more likely to respond to risk than they are to change for change's sake.

Your risk-management plan might look something like this (see opposite page).

If you're in the middle of an unplanned disaster at work, get your team together, use some of the techniques discussed in principle 5 and host a team meeting. It only needs to be about an hour or so. Bring food or wine if it's awful. Ask the questions – 'What's possible here? How can we make it happen? What are our other options? What are we assuming? What could be possible?'

Risk-management plan

Project Name					
Prepared By					
Date:					
Identified Risk	**Analysis**			**Treatment**	**Responsibility**
	Probability (1–5)	Impact (1–5)	Rank (1–5)		

You, as a leader, might be feeling a little scared to take the initiative and do something different. Start small and have a go by making a small change to the plan. I've found that action, doing something, generally breeds confidence, and then you might feel more confident to have another go at another change.

CONCLUSION

Heartfelt leadership is both an art and a science. So is project management. Adopting a project-management philosophy allows a heartfelt leader to get things done. Our masculine skill set reinforces the need for responsibility, action and accountability to get things done. Our feminine skill set embraces our ability to innovate, create and lead change. Do both.

You, as a leader, might like to be in control because you feel that that's how a good leader behaves – whereas a great leader will encourage change. This tension requires you to get comfortable with the uncomfortable.

Paraphrasing the thoughts of David Deida, 'The way of man or woman is control. The way of the universe is chaos.' It is on you, as a heartfelt leader, to find the right tempo and balance between order and chaos (you need both). But never forget! A lack of accountability lets people off the hook and descends you into chaos; whereas an organisation that is tightly controlled stifles innovation and change.

You need to look to your projects and people and look for opportunities for both control and chaos, because chaos breeds change for us.

In the next chapter, you will learn how to make your team members love you to bits when you feed them exactly what they want.

7

Feed your team their favourite food

When I started this book, I wanted to share how to fix stuff and be a better leader, and show you the tricks you would need to feel more confident about yourself. I wanted to show you what I've learned in my journey and the many practical things I can teach you. However, I realised along the way that heartfelt leadership goes deeper than just the practical. I've learned that most of us want something more, something deeper – from our lives, jobs and relationships. Guess what? So does your team.

This chapter explores what your team wants from you. Not knowing what your team wants can be scary because you are moving from a traditional leadership model – of control – to a heartfelt leadership model – of trust. This chapter is about communicating the information your team wants and not what you want them to know. As a heartfelt leader, you will still need to get things done; I am not saying that you should let the plan be all about them. Your plan must deliver your strategic goals AND engage with the personal needs and beliefs of your team.

As a heartfelt leader, you will learn to balance your masculine skill set of getting things done with your feminine skill set of sharing stories with your people. Sharing stories is what helps us to connect and feel united. If you only focus on the tasks and getting things done, your team will quickly feel like a cog in a machine.

TELL THEM WHAT THEY WANT TO KNOW

You, like me, might fall into the trap of listening to your own ego and self-importance. And, it is only with the benefit of hindsight that you can see it, and yourself, for what it really is. This is a common mistake when we focus on the task at hand and not the people in the room.

Just recently, I was leading a decision-making process with my own team. I was the kingpin in a tender-writing process for our new business and I was totally focused on winning the prize. The official prize being winning significant new work and cash for our start up.

Of course, the unofficial prize was the stroking of my own ego and the validation and recognition that would come with the win. But more about that later. I assembled a room full of experts. Finance people. Plant operators. Admin support. The maintenance manager. Then I proceeded to spin them through all the things that I needed from them to get the tender lodged.

Now remember, I have 20-plus years of technical experience in building, writing and winning tenders. But, my room had less than five minutes of experience.

I talk fast. I act fast and I think fast. And, in record time I lost them. I was met with stunned silence and polite commentary. The only input or participation I received was some animated conversations about the type of truck we would buy in the future to meet the needs of the job.

This, post meeting, left me in tears of rage and frustration. And working on a Sunday to clean up the mess, and building a pile of self-righteous resentment. That, in my opinion, my team could be so stupid, so inept and so unorganised was completely under my skin. And, because old habits die hard, I found myself doing the job alone.

Later, once the job was done, I was able to reflect on the mess and debrief with my Craig. I had waltzed into the room totally focused on the task. *Get the tender done.* And not for one minute had I considered the audience. I had failed to think about what the room needed from me. In doing so I had alienated my support.

You might have experienced something similar – a situation where you spent a heap of energy on a task in preparation for a meeting and then wondered why nobody got on board and got as excited as you about your project, so the meeting fell flat.

My team simply got, from me, the technical wizardry that I had spent the best part of my career cultivating. Unfortunately, I had failed to serve my team their favourite food – which was what they needed to know. The meeting became all about me and not about them at all.

In this chapter, I will explore the importance of understanding what's going on for your team. One of your jobs as a heartfelt leader is to understand what is happening for each individual: where are they at, and what do they need? And, you need to roll this up into how this is influencing the collective team. With a better under-standing of what is going on for your team members, you will be better able to deliver what they need to know.

I am also going to cover the tension point between sharing and doing. Specifically, we'll look at:

- Sharing the doing by recognising the value of a love-in, which is a cheeky term for a facilitated workshop with your team.

- Recognising the effort and countering the 'We didn't know that' message you might receive from your team.

- Heartfelt one-to-ones – some coaching stories about how you can get the best out of your people.

SHARING THE DOING

Some of my clients have instigated exceptional love-ins as a result of our work together. They've told me of meetings that have changed the culture of their organisation or fixed big problems. But, how often have you sat in a meeting with your team, only to hear people saying things like, 'I didn't know that that was happening'?

You might be perplexed by this feedback because, these days, we have so many different communication tools. But unfortunately, the right noises won't always get through to your team.

I want you to think about the old 'what's in it for me?' principle. Most of what you're communicating with your team should be about *what your team wants from you* – NOT about your achievements, problems or tasks. Your team is looking for two essential things from you:

1. *Clarity* on where they are going

2. *The opportunity to share* what they're doing towards that goal.

Poor preparation

In principle 3 I shared a story about the witch who I wanted my mate, Sandy, to help me sort out with a pitchfork. I was so enraged that this lady, the witch, dared to criticise the delivery of my workshop that I tried to enlist Sandy to help take her down. But the absolute truth about that story was that I, as a workshop facilitator, delivered what I wanted to tell the audience about leadership, with little regard for the room's needs. The witch's feedback was on point: my preparation was inadequate for the workshop. In this chapter, I am going to explore how you fix that.

Bringing your team together, whether you're doing it face-to-face or in the new world via Zoom, is an expensive exercise. People are away from their jobs and are committing their time to you. You want to make the sessions count, and you want to build the culture of your team in the right direction because if you don't, then frankly, it can be a waste of time and money.

We didn't know

Over my 20 years as a coach and facilitator, I've been fortunate to work with hundreds of teams across a diverse range of industries. The most common complaint that I receive, particularly when I'm running a strategic planning session and no matter what the industry – manufacturing, health, health services, business or community development – are 'We don't know what's going on' and 'Communication here is abysmal.'

Complaints about poor communication quickly escalate to judgement about what the boss or the leader is doing well or not. From there, it's a quick jump to describing them as poor leaders. I often wonder what is happening underneath all these complaints, because it's easy to complain that communication is poor. People want to be heard and share what they're doing. The agenda and preparation need to reflect what your people need from you, not the other way around.

As a leader, you might be wondering, 'How will I ever get anything done if I make it all about them?' Human nature is to be self-driven. If you can link where you are going with your team members' own needs, you'll get to your destination a whole bunch faster.

As a heartfelt leader, you still need to get things done. Don't let the agenda be all about them – instead, craft your agenda in a way that achieves the strategic goals of your business or the project by linking the tasks and your team's tasks and actions to a commonly understood need.

Activity 25: Your love-in

I've called it a love-in which is a cheeky and sarcastic term. But what I am talking about is pulling your team together for a meeting. And then doing some proper preparation in advance for that meeting with your team. It's not about slapping an agenda together in a rushed meeting request. It takes time and some intuitive thinking.

As a heartfelt leader, you should ask yourself some critical questions in your preparation. For example:

- What do we need to achieve at a business level?

- What are my team members' concerns?

- What roadblocks are holding us back?

- How can I link the business goals to the individual goals of my team members?

- What do I need to understand from my team's perspective?

Once you've done that work yourself, you will be clear about the preparation you need to do, and you will have the answers to structure your agenda. It might now look something like:

1. A debrief from the team.

    a. What are you most proud of?

    b. Where are we at with a particular project?

2. The Good, the Bad and the Ugly (see activity 26).

3. Where are we going next?

    Most importantly, provide food or wine in the meeting!

Activity 26: **The Good, the Bad and the Ugly**

One of my favourite facilitation techniques, which I call the Good, the Bad and the Ugly, is a valuable feedback mechanism for your team. This model allows people to talk about what's going really well (the Good); what needs improvement – the things that we need to fix (the Bad); and the dirty stuff that we have to get on the table to understand where we're at (the Ugly). It gives people the freedom to express themselves objectively: 'This is what's happening.'

You might feel that, as the leader, you need to have all of the answers and control the meeting. But a heartfelt leader can be prepared by knowing their stuff, doing the prep work and trusting that they can lead and facilitate the conversation.

RECOGNISING THE EFFORT

In your career, there may have been times when you haven't felt recognised for the effort you put in. How did that feel for you? Did it motivate you to do more? My guess is probably not. It probably had the opposite effect, where you became demotivated because you didn't feel appreciated. Guess what? Your team likely feels the same.

An attentive leader is a powerful glue for a team. Being engaged is also essential for promoting a feeling of connection and motivation within your team.

Messenger conflict

I'm the vice president of our local netball club. Previous to that, I was the president of our netball club. I've spent a lot of time around a large volunteer base. These are great people with great energy and, in the modern world, about a dozen Facebook Messenger groups. All of the individual teams have a Messenger group each, the committee has a Messenger group, the executive has a Messenger group and the coaches have a Messenger group. Communication across the club happens as a team, by structure and on a daily and hourly basis. Often, it's overwhelming trying to keep up with all of the communication that's firing around.

I've noticed that conflict inevitably arises because people are reading the comments and threads at different times of the day. People also tend to read the message threads as either a question or a criticism of their effort – whereas often, the sender only wants to clarify what is going on. Over the years, I've asked that we minimise our conversations in Messenger and use it simply as a noticeboard for what's happening. I have also noticed that the heavier the reliance on Messenger, the more likely there are to be hurt feelings because people take the commentary out of context or out of intent. I've found Messenger to be a dangerous tool that often is misused inadvertently. And there are a bunch of apps and communication tools just like this.

Activity 27: Time to shine

It is a lot of effort to organise your team, and you might want to argue that people should do their job without acknowledgement. 'I don't need to recognise everything that they're doing,' you might think.

Turn that around and think about it from your perspective and how you would feel after a significant project. I bet that you would want to celebrate and acknowledge what a journey, what an effort your project/event/thing has been for you and the people around you.

That said, when you tune into your team and what's going on, you need to be mindful that you don't go too granular. You don't want to become too excessive in your attention because otherwise, it becomes meaningless. For example, you don't need to ask your team member how they're going every time you walk past them.

Instead, ask your team members to run part of the agenda by delivering a section on their own project. However, be specific about the guidelines at your team love-in. You might like to give each person, or project, a time allocation of 10 minutes. Most people can't keep to their time allocation once they start talking about their project. Be tough on them in terms of timekeeping. Give them some guidelines about what they need to share and what you want to hear about their project. This might include:

- What's working

- What's not working

- What resources they need

- What could change

- What they're learning about their project.

  Critical questions for you to then ask might include:

- What has been your greatest challenge?

- Why is it important to you?

- Why is it important to us?

- What support do you need from us?

Be specific about the timeframe your team has for their presentation. You will also need a strong chair – yourself or somebody else – to facilitate the conversation so that people stay on point and share what needs to be shared.

You might be nervous about handing over parts of your agenda to your team. It could be risky. What if they use it as an opportunity to derail the meeting with criticism? My experience has been that more often than not, given a chance to present their project, your team will put a heap of effort into their preparation because they want to share, and they want the recognition of the hard work that they've put in. It will be the opposite – you will be trying to rein in the amount of information they want to share. You'll need to keep the boundaries very clear.

HEARTFELT ONE-TO-ONES

As a heartfelt leader, you walk the line every day between being a practical problem-solver who makes things happen, and an intuitive coach of human behaviour who is constantly seeking to grow and learn from personal experience and the team's shared experience. As a business and executive coach, I've had the good fortune to work one-to-one with many great leaders. While my clients come to me with a list of problems that we can fix, once we triage the problem, we often find much more going on – something much deeper that needs work.

Your job as a heartfelt leader is to seek out the problems and fix them. Then, when the time's right, dig a little deeper and find out what is happening for this human and their journey.

People will follow you wherever you want to go if they trust you.

The power of one-to-one

My husband and I run and operate three separate but integrated businesses employing more than 35 people. Our business growth has happened pretty quickly, in the space of about five years. Across our businesses, the single most powerful thing that we do is hold regular one-to-ones with our key leadership team members. In turn, those leaders hold one-to-ones with their people.

In our one-to-ones, we have the opportunity, within a predetermined agenda, to work through what's happening at a business level, a team level and a personal level with our key leaders.

You might think that you don't have the right coaching skills to take a job like this. But humans want to talk about themselves and what they're working on to make sure they matter. Give your team members the time and the space to open up. Ask them some good questions about what's going on for them. Back in principle 5 we looked at success-based questions. The question that stands out for me here is to remember to ask, 'How can we fix something?' rather than, 'Why did that happen?'

But remember, you are not a psychologist. You might not have the skills to fix the big stuff. It's your job, however, to unearth the issue. You can help your team members identify what is holding them back from their full potential. That's what this whole book is about – unearthing the deeper tensions that exist inside your team and your people so that you can help them to realise their full potential.

As you move through this work of a heartfelt leader, you will come up against some tough stuff with people who might be experiencing mental ill health or deeply traumatic psychological issues. Show grace and support to your team members, and help them connect to the relevant mental health professional that can support them through whatever's going on. Then you can keep your role as a heartfelt leader separate from their psychological process.

Activity 28: Holding a meaningful one-to-one

Schedule regular one-to-ones with each of your key leaders. Choose a regular time, place and timeframe, and put it in your diary. Set up an agenda similar to your team's love-in agenda. The key questions that you'll be asking your leaders will be:

- What important work are you doing?
- What important work have you finished?
- Why is it important to you?
- Why is it important to us?
- What support do you need from me right now?
- What is keeping you awake at night?

A one-to-one is the most critical heartfelt leadership task that you can have with your team. You'll build the trust that you need slowly but gradually. As the trust between you and your key leader develops, you will go progressively deeper and deeper with them.

As a leader, you might feel uncomfortable getting up close and personal with your team members. Do it slowly because they'll feel a little awkward as well. The first time your boss asks you what's keeping you awake at night, you'll be suspicious. Go at it gently.

Keep your professional barriers clear. Gradually build trust with your team members and then go deeper. You might like to reacquaint yourself with some of the success questions we talked about back in principle 5. A great open question around the difference between feedback and failure that you could use here is, 'What did you learn from this experience?' Alternatively, you might like to use the curiosity versus assumptions framework that we talked about and say, 'I'm curious to know what you think about this.' These gentle questions allow the person to open up without you having to ask them straight out, 'What's going on for you?'

CONCLUSION

In this chapter, we have explored the realities of being a human.

We all like to talk about ourselves and what we have achieved.

And sometimes, as a leader, you will do that to your team. You will drown them, like I did with my technical skill. True heartfelt leaders will turn the tables and consider how this impacts the needs of the people around them when they share what they're doing.

I still struggle with overwhelming my team, but I am now more mindful about how I present information. I focus on the learning and development opportunities for my team, and ask myself, 'What does the production manager need from this conversation? What does the admin team need?' I consciously slow down my pace, take the time to think about the bigger picture and seek to understand what other people need.

You are human, and you have grown up with leadership models that suggest you have to be correct and have all the answers. Moving your mindset from a need to control to a need to trust will be among the scariest things you've ever done as a human and leader.

As an evolving heartfelt leader, practise linking business goals to the individual needs of your team members. Rather than forcing your company's will onto people in your charge, help them identify where they fit so they can choose to either get on the bus or get off, depending on where it's going for them.

Above all, remember that if you communicate what your team wants to know, you will have them far more engaged. On the other hand, if you focus your communication on what you want to tell them, you might just end up with more happening in Messenger than you want.

There's nothing like a party to get everyone's attention. In the next chapter, I will share with you how we can party like there's no tomorrow.

8

Celebrate success because life is short

As I've written this book, it's made me think about how I could help you: the evolving, heartfelt leader. I started practical and gave you specific tasks, tricks and tips – stuff to get you out of a jam and help you move forward. But if you've been listening, you know that you, me, us, we all need to go deeper. Do you have enough quiet moments? Moments where you can ponder things like life, trust, connection and what's next?

In the meantime, let me help you, on a practical level, to sort your shit out and get more and better stuff done with less fuss. If you are brave, let's talk about the big stuff, the hard stuff, because here's the kicker: we're all going to be dead soon, so let's enjoy the ride.

In my lifetime, I have been described as all sorts of things. My early school report cards include commentary like, 'Kerry is a sensitive girl who gets herself worried.' Like you, I've lost people on my journey. I've lost a best friend and my identity a few times over.

And when my health has declined, my body has needed to remind me what is important.

When you acknowledge that life is short, you have two choices. The first choice is to numb this reality with any avoidance technique that you can find, including food, alcohol, sex, work or drugs. The second choice is to adopt a heartfelt approach to tune in to your feminine skill set and storytelling abilities and reflect on what you have learned. You can balance this with your masculine skill set: your ability to create, produce and leave a legacy. This chapter explores your ability to reflect and then also look forward and create a legacy.

Life is precious, and life is short. All of us should live life to the full, with no regrets.

THE BIG C

This family of mine has had many challenges. My husband Craig lost his forever love to the big C, cancer, several years ago. He was married to Jody, who developed adrenal cancer. Jody brought three children to their relationship from her two previous marriages. When Jody and Craig got together, they had a baby – Chelsea, my stepdaughter.

Jody and Craig walked the road of adrenal cancer together. It was a shitty, heartbreaking thing. And it was the making of a man who relentlessly pursued every option that he had to save his love from cancer. When those options were exhausted, he accepted the reality of it all with grace. He came home, took his children into his arms and delivered the news. Brick by brick, he supported his family while nursing his loss. He embraced life as Jody would have wanted it and set out to #lovelife.

Sometime after Jody passed away, Craig and I got together. Between us, we have six children who have four dads. From those six children, we also have five grandchildren. It has been the making of both of us – we have both travelled our own roads to arrive at this point. It makes us appreciate how fragile life is and how we should celebrate life every day because we never know what's around the corner.

As heartfelt leaders, we walk the line, and we embrace the balance. We find the bits that work for us. When we acknowledge just how precious life is, we're faced with two choices – to numb this reality or live life to the full. I want you (and me) to take the second choice and embrace your heartfelt leadership and the balance between your feminine skill set and your masculine skill set.

I want you to tell your teams and your family stories and plant trees under whose shade you will never sit.

In this chapter, I'm going to talk about reflection and legacy, putting a full stop on things so that you can move forward, honouring your life lessons and celebrating a life well-lived.

I will also discuss celebration as the practice that will bind us together as reflective storytellers and legacy leavers.

REFLECTION AND LEGACY

As a heartfelt leader, you know that things will go wrong, and you plan for it, as I showed you back in principle 2. As we talked about in principle 4, you know that honest conversations with real people are hard, but they get better results. You also understand that you get more things done when you reframe your language and use success-based words rather than stuck words, as we talked about in principle 5.

Despite all this, bad things happen to good people. As a heartfelt leader, you will learn to accept this so that you don't live in an old story forever. Sometimes you need to put a full stop to a disaster so that you can move forward.

Burning shit

In my 30s when I was a self-employed project manager, I worked on some good projects and some shitty projects with a team of seven. At the end of a particularly shitty project – a complex strategic planning process that had run for most of the year and involved a demanding customer and a difficult outcome – we needed to put a full stop on that project.

I organised a formal debrief. We sat down together and collected the learnings, using the feedback techniques I talked about in principle 7. I also organised some drinks and some food and we had some fun. Once the formal bit was over, I took my team into the courtyard at the back of our office, where a fire pit was ready. I took out the strategic plan that we'd written. This plan had taken us more than six months, included more than 20 individual pieces of community consultation and workshops, and the effort of seven people. And piece by piece, I fed that few hundred pages of work into the fire pit. It was cathartic and a symbolic end for both me and my team because it had been such a challenging project. It was nice to put a full stop on it and leave it there. That then gave us the freedom to move forward onto the next project.

You might feel like you can't let go of the pain, the trauma, the frustration or the stress, and nor can your team. Reframe the problem or the stress point into, 'What did we learn from this process?' and then eat the cake.

We are all going to be challenged by life at some point in our journey. However, at different times, you will identify people around you who are struggling mentally and possibly have mental health issues that need professional support. Help them help themselves by connecting them to good mental health professionals. Your leadership at this time may help them to do this gracefully and promptly.

Activity 29: Your team debrief

At the end of every big project, every milestone, every job, host a team meeting. Set the time, set the day, organise food and wine, and run a session where you debrief. The tool that I use is called Plus, Minus and Interesting (PMI). It's a project-management technique that collects the positive, negative and interesting aspects of a project during a debrief.

And yep, for those of you who are paying attention, this is a very similar technique to the Good, the Bad and the Ugly detailed back in activity 26.

Keep the debrief simple but allow yourselves to move forward. What were the good things that happened in this project? What were the things that were frustrating or challenging? What were some of the interesting things? It's the act of recording it, reflecting on it and then moving forward that counts.

Sometimes we get frustrated and disappointed that things didn't go to plan. Please keep it in perspective by remembering that life is short. Ask yourself, 'Will this matter in five years?'

HONOURING YOUR LIFE LESSONS

Life will give you hundreds of growth opportunities as a heartfelt leader – for yourself and the people around you. Honouring those life lessons is simply another way to turn your events or things into stories that help you and others grow. In turn, your stories help you to create the clarity that you need to craft your legacy. You can begin by asking yourself, 'How do I want to write the story? How do I want to write this chapter?'

In every event, experience or problem, there's a silver lining. It's up to you, as a heartfelt leader, to find the hidden lesson.

A little bit of spew

Earlier I introduced the notion that I was a very sensitive child, and I've found that helpful at times when I've been coaching my team.

Mum kept all our report cards from school, and when I read back on my report cards, I see commentary along the lines of, 'Kerry is a sensitive girl. Kerry can get anxious.'

The best example of how that played out for me as an adult was my first day at work. I was a country kid who spent my life in a country community. The school bus used to pick me up from and drop me off at the front gate. I travelled with people I knew to a school I knew. When I left home, I moved to Adelaide, to the city, and started a new job in the then Department of Transport. The enormous anxiety on my first day of work was catching the metropolitan bus to work. I was terrified that I was going to miss the bus stop. You had to pull the cord to ring the bell in those days, and the bus would stop. I wasn't worried about going to work, but I was concerned about getting on a bus full of strangers and then having the ability to pull the bell at the right time and get off.

I was so anxious about the bus ride that, on the morning of my first day of work, I got myself into such a lather that I decided I needed to throw up as I was walking out the door. I cleaned myself up, and then I eventually got to the bus stop and got to work without incident. I spent an enjoyable morning meeting my new team, finding my desk and getting settled. I was having a great day, until about lunchtime when I looked down on my flash new blouse, and I saw a little blob of spew still sitting there.

From that day, I have learned that anxiety should not inhibit my life choices; instead, the fear or nerves is a gift that guides me. I know something's important to me because I feel anxious about it.

You might be thinking, 'What if I can't find the lesson?' Maybe you can't see it yet. Give it time. It might take a few years, but with hindsight, you'll see the lesson. In the meantime, ask yourself some questions.

In my case, you could ask, 'What is the hidden benefit of my anxiety?' Or, 'What did or didn't happen because I was doing this?' The hidden benefit of my anxiety is that it teaches me when something is important to me, but it also makes me sensitive to people's feelings. I can tune in when other people are feeling anxious, and that makes me a better leader.

What did or didn't happen because I was doing this? On that day, when I started work, I'd chosen to take a job because it was the late 1980s and the country was in high recession. Rather than going to uni, I took a job. If I'd gone to uni, I would have studied accounting and likely never indulged my creativity. Thank the lord that I didn't do accounting because it would have been horrific to spend my life with numbers. My passion for words and pictures would have drowned under the weight of those numbers. So I consider that I was blessed to be on the bus that day, going to a job where I learned a whole heap of other skills.

Activity 30: Rewriting your story

Turn your hardships into lessons. Grab yourself a journal – an actual book, something with a beautiful hardcover and blank pages that's got a lovely tactile feel about it. Get yourself a nice pen and find yourself a quiet spot at home or in the garden, and write the hardship down as you remember it. You don't need to censor it, and you should include all of the shitty stuff. This journal is for your eyes only. Get as dirty and terrible as you need to about things that hurt you and make you angry. Get it all out, and then let it simmer for a couple of days. Then come back to it later with fresh eyes and ask yourself:

- What were the hidden benefits of this event?
- What did or didn't happen because I was doing this?

Once you've done that, rewrite the story or the event. Rewrite it as if you were teaching your children a lesson. Focus on the hidden learnings and craft them into a story. Don't stress about how rough it is – the spelling, the prose, the words. It's your journal and your story. The outcome that you're looking for is, 'What did I learn from that hardship?'

You might think that journaling is a bit weird or that you don't like writing. But it's not about how you write or what you write. It's the thinking that's the significant bit. You don't have to share it with anybody.

CELEBRATING A LIFE WELL-LIVED

In *Ferris Bueller's Day Off*, Ferris Bueller says, 'Life moves pretty fast. If you don't stop and look around once in a while, you could miss it.' Covid-19 has taught me that as well. Life was super busy, and then I had the great reset, where I learned to connect with my family, plant some trees and slow down the pace to enjoy the things that mattered. I want to encourage you to take the time to reflect, celebrate and consider what legacy you want to leave with your team, your family and for yourself.

We're all ageing and moving towards an indefinite future. Take the time to celebrate your achievements now.

Tell the story

In principle 3, I shared how vital my friend Sandy was to me and how she taught me to own my own shit and face the mirror. Sandy also taught me so much more. She taught me the value of mates, barbecues, catch-ups, deep conversations and stupid activities. Sandy was the friend who organised people and parties for no other reason than it was fun.

On the day I delivered her eulogy, I wrote a piece about what she meant to me and what I learned from her. What sticks with me from that is the genesis of this book and the genesis of heartfelt leadership: 'If I had not told the story and celebrated a life well-lived, I would not be here today, writing this for you. Sandy's story was a short one but a good one. And if that's not a reason to drink vodka out of a jam jar, then I don't know what is.'

The funeral was hard going. And then we had the wake afterwards. The wake involved a lot of alcohol and tears and concluded with me ordering a shot. Sandy was a lover of shots, and I'm not. I can't tolerate mixing alcohol, but Sandy was a demon at a party, bringing out the shots and then mixing the shots.

I often wondered whether she was making the shots but then not drinking them herself, but she just had a tremendous capacity for alcohol so that she could drink shot after shot. Usually, that ended up with me in the garden, sick because I couldn't tolerate it. On the day of her funeral, I decided that I should have a shot of vodka in her honour at the end of the wake, but they had run out of shot glasses. The bartender poured me a shot of vodka in one of those fancy jam jars. Do you know those big wide jars that were all the rage for a while? Then my family watched with horror as I did a shot from the jam jar. The day unwound pretty dramatically after that.

The moral of this story is to celebrate a life well-lived and occasionally drink vodka out of a jam jar.

Activity 31: Celebrate. A lot.

You might not have the budget for fancy celebrations at work, or your team members are in different places – working at home, in different states or across the world. But Covid-19 has taught us that we can get creative. In 2020, we did Friday night drinks by Zoom. It could just be something small and simple to celebrate milestones. But, make sure you drink responsibly!

The celebration does not need to be expensive – and often, the cheesier the festival, the better. Brainstorm a list of possible celebrations that you can do with your team. Here's a list to get you started:

- Donuts for everyone when we hit our target.

- Free drinks at the quarter-end.

- Boss for a day – reward a team member with the title of being the boss and give them the authority for the day.

- Plastic trophies for finish-line parties: 'We made it.'

- Lunch in the park, where you bring your lunch and sit in the sun.

- A visit to your other worksites to see the impact of your efforts.

- Volunteering at a local community group, aged care centre or kindy – you can give back somewhere else.

Your creativity might be holding you back. Ask your team for ideas. It doesn't have to be about money or lavish celebrations. It can simply be something fun.

CONCLUSION

Our influence as leaders is temporary. We're all ageing and changing every day.

You are here for a finite amount of time; you don't know how long that is.

Please make the most of it. Create a culture of fun, and celebrate the wins and losses. Consider what stories you want to tell your grandchildren about the things that you did.

Take the time to pause; take the time and the opportunity to reflect; and take the time to build your legacy. At the highest level, I'm asking you to be intentional about your life and consciously create your gift to the world.

Enjoy life. Life is fun, and we should equally celebrate the good and the bad.

Life can feel like a movie, such as *The Hunger Games*, where the game master controls you. In the next chapter, you are the game master.

Leadership is not focusing on one thing at a time...

GUY DOWNES ©

... but addressing multiple things all at once.

officeguycartoons.com

9

Know that life is an iterative process

Life, leadership and projects are not linear processes that get easier with practice. They are iterative processes. As a project manager, I lived for my utopian world of control and order in my early days. More recently, in my transition to a heartfelt leader, I've learned that life doesn't go the way that we planned – and that's okay.

This principle is the most important yet. It is about balance. Not the mystical balance that you might have been sold back in the 1980s with the mystique that you could have it all: work, life, kids, community, health and sex. I am talking about personal and real inner balance, where you embrace your most profound truth as a leader and utilise both your masculine and feminine skill sets.

This principle is where it all comes together and where you learn how you can find your inner balance as a leader by applying the right combination of masculine and feminine skills for you.

You do this through iteration – project iteration, leadership iteration and life iteration.

When you accept that projects, leadership and life are all about iteration, you adopt a philosophy that leadership is about learning, change and growth. As a heartfelt leader, you come to understand that knowledge, change and growth fuels your achievement of lots of little goals along the way, which will ultimately make up your legacy.

ENERGETIC ADJUSTMENT

In my late 30s I found myself as a single parent, and it was the destruction of my ideological picket fence. I then adopted a masculine approach to life where I became the protector, provider, nurturer and supporter in my family. That put me out of balance. I overdid the masculine skill set. I became all about control and order, and I lost a lot of my empathy and creativity.

Later, when I remarried, I was able to rethink my masculine and feminine skill sets. This change in energy enabled me to reintroduce my feminine skills and allow what I call polarity in the relationship – two of us who complement each other with our masculine and feminine skill sets.

This book is not about belting the patriarchy, or sinning the sisterhood. It is about finding the right skills to set the balance as you progress through your life and leadership roles.

Throughout this book, I've been looking at the complementary masculine/feminine skill sets so that you can explore your most profound truth or deepest reality as a leader. This principle explores the polarities and complementarities of both the masculine and feminine skill sets in leaders. First, I will look at the masculine and feminine – and how it relates to project management being an iterative process. Next, I will discuss leadership's masculine and feminine skill sets and leadership as an iterative process. Finally,

I will talk about life's masculine and feminine skill sets and how life is an iterative process.

MASCULINE AND FEMININE: PROJECT MANAGEMENT IS AN ITERATIVE PROCESS

As you know, I'm a project manager by trade. For more than 20 years, I've coached project management clients. You might be like some of those clients, coming to me and asking, 'How do I get my team to do more of the right stuff?' Or you might be frustrated by questions like, 'Why don't my people do what they say they will?' This frustration is genuine. The paradox of leadership is wanting your people to take responsibility to get the stuff done versus making sure that they're doing the right stuff.

One of the most painful lessons I learned in my early project management days – pretty much like the day I learned that the Tooth Fairy isn't real – was that project management is a change-management process. For it to be genuinely successful, project management is an iterative process. Stuff happens, so no matter how good your project-management plans are, you will need to change them as you go. I'm not talking about poor project planning and surprises. I'm talking about good, solidly researched plans that are progressively adapted to suit the reality of a new situation that you didn't anticipate.

Project management is art (a feminine skill set) and science (a masculine skill set). Within projects, it's easy to get focused on logic: the science of time, and cost and schedule. But a truly successful project manager also understands that humans need care, consideration, empathy, creativity and innovation to bring a project to life. The genuinely skilful and gifted project managers are those who innately understand the need to walk the line between their feminine and masculine skill sets.

When you accept that things will change as your project and team mature, you can manage that change more gracefully and successfully. If you are like me in my early days and stick rigidly to the plan, you'll be left behind when the change happens.

Start. Plan. Do. Finish.

As a practising project manager, I taught project management to hundreds of people for about ten years. The most common desire for all of my students was to manage a project perfectly so that things didn't go wrong and, more importantly, they didn't get blamed for the mistakes. Many of them would come to me with a pretty straightforward story. It went something like this: they had a conversation with their boss in the tea room; the boss assigned them to the project; they were so excited to be given the project that they rushed back to their desk and started looking at their diary to work out how they were going to fit it in. They jumped straight into the start phase without thinking.

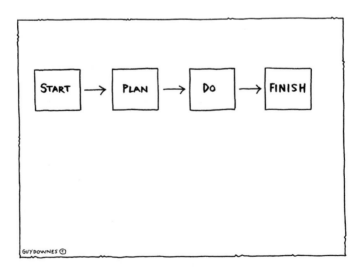

GUY DOWNES ©

128

But, what they were actually doing was spending less than 5 per cent of their time in the 'start' phase. A new project manager will rapidly move into planning mode and pull out an Excel sheet or a diary, and spend less than 10 per cent of their project time in the 'plan' phase if they're lucky. They're scheduling meetings, buying resources, organising things and making things happen. Their planning is lightning quick, which means they move into what we call the 'do' phase extremely fast.

And because they've planned the project poorly and haven't considered all the options, they spend most of their waking time putting out fires. They spend 80 per cent or more of their energy rushing around, sorting the project out and doing the project. Inevitably, it ends in tears. They're disappointed, or the boss is disappointed, or the client's disappointed. They finish up the project as quickly as possible, and they don't take the learnings, they don't document, they don't archive. They move on quickly.

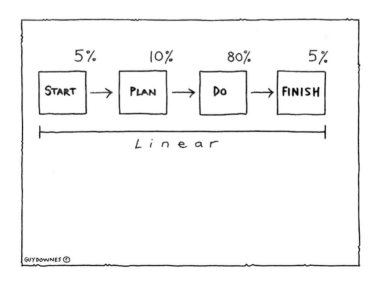

129

Pain happens for new project managers because they so quickly jump into the 'do' phase because they haven't thought through or asked about where the project's going. At this point, they show up at my class, looking for advice on fixing it.

You might be thinking, 'I'm not a project manager; I'm a leader.' But we are all project managers, no matter our title. Project managers engage resources and people to make things happen. And because of this I want you to understand the iterative nature of project management to support your understanding of the iterative nature of leadership.

As a project manager of any level, you engage your planning skill set (masculine skill set) together with your creativity skill set (feminine skill set) to improve your projects by investing more time in the things that matter and changing where you spend your energy.

Activity 32: **Project iteration**

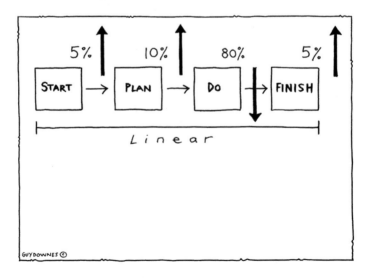

So how do you iterate a project? How can you improve that phase at the start of the project? You begin by increasing the amount of time you're spending in the 'start' phase. You invest your energy into conversations with the key people to ensure that everyone is clear about what you want out of the project. Moving forward, you then have a clearer understanding of where you, and your team, are going.

Also increase your time spent in the 'plan' phase, and put well more than 10 per cent of your overall effort into planning. Again invest your energy into the conversations with those key people to understand how you will deliver the project step-by-step, what's going on and how you can manage it.

Move away from being the project doer. You should not be the person doing the project, but rather acting as a project leader. Identify the issues, problems and wins, and adjusting your project accordingly. The 'do' phase is where iteration becomes critical. As you move into the project, you are constantly making minor adjustments – the reiteration of the iterations to the project plan – to deliver a successful project rather than being reactive.

As you move into the 'finish' phase of the project, increase the amount of time you spend debriefing the project so that you're reviewing the delivery, learnings and key recordings before you move on to something new.

But here is the real trick. It is not just about spending more time in the 'start' phase or the 'plan' phase, it is actually about constantly iterating the project as new information comes to light. Meaning your project lifecycle will look more like this, than the utopian project-management dream of a linear, perfectly organised project.

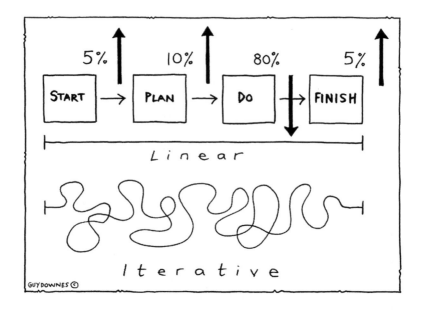

At this point you might be thinking, 'I don't have the tools or project management experience that's required to manage a project.' I promise, good project management is based on good communication, not fancy apps or tools. And if you use the communication techniques in principle 7 and the accountability techniques in principle 6 you will have the raw information you need to successfully manage your projects and team.

MASCULINE AND FEMININE: LEADERSHIP IS AN ITERATIVE PROCESS

Like project management, leadership is very much an iterative process. It's not a set-and-forget model. Leadership requires more than one conversation. It requires many conversations to check and re-check that you understand your team's perspective. As a heartfelt leader, your job is to continue the evolution or the iteration every day to lead and grow your team.

A heartfelt approach to leadership is not about masculine or feminine skill sets being right or wrong. It recognises that leadership is iterative and that we learn as we go. There's no perfect day of arrival where you get it all right. You get the lesson about how to improve as you move forward.

My leadership iteration

In my journey as a heartfelt leader, I've felt the tension between a masculine approach and a feminine approach. In principle 8, I shared the feedback from my earlier teachers that 'Kerry is a sensitive child' and 'Kerry worries too much.' Maybe, like you, I thought that to be successful, I needed to overcome or manage my emotions so that I would fit in. Once I hit the workplace in the late 1980s, I found that the blokes were in charge, and I quickly learned that masculine skills – getting the job done, completion, perfection, no mistakes on the job – were the currency for success.

I solidified my masculine leadership approach in my years as a single parent, project manager and business owner. These were the days where I learned to be all-in on a masculine leadership model. I kept it all about the task, the job, the outcome, the result and the win.

A marriage breakdown, a minor health crisis and the loss of my best mate Sandy triggered a realisation that perhaps there was a better, more heartfelt way. My second marriage now provides me with endless opportunities to test this theorem, but more about that later.

You might be thinking, 'I'm not buying the masculine/feminine argument. It sounds like you want to make the blokes bad or the women right.' Think back to your career and to the people who truly helped your growth and development. Who was instrumental? Maybe the leaders who were compassionate and empathetic to your situation and equally kept you accountable to the task were the more instrumental leaders?

The heartfelt leadership model is not a feminist debate. It's about adapting our skill sets to the environment at hand.

Activity 33: Leadership timeline

To illustrate this point, I encourage you to timeline your career journey and identify the most influential leaders for you. Then take a moment and think about your growth and learning as a leader. Where have you iterated your leadership style along the way?

To do this, grab a large sheet of paper and a pack of coloured markers. Draw a timeline, starting with when you first started work – your first job, second job, industry change, whatever happened for you. Then identify, by year or milestone, some of the key leaders who came and went. Write down their name and their characteristics. Think about the positive and negative role models you met along the way, and list what you learned from those leaders.

Now, look at that list and consider the masculine and feminine traits in the list. Ask yourself which traits you might have adopted yourself and which you could adopt as you move forward.

You might have been in a situation where you have had terrible leaders, terrible bosses or terrible experiences along the way. Look for the learning. What did these people and experiences teach you about how you want to be as a leader? Flip the coin and look at the things you learned about how you *don't* want to behave.

MASCULINE AND FEMININE: LIFE IS AN ITERATIVE PROCESS

Since time immemorial, humans have philosophised about the meaning of life and why we are here. Yet you, like me, might want to know how to survive *this week*. How can you get through your agenda and get stuff done?

Balancing your energies

All philosophers have attempted to unravel the meaning of life. As mere mortals and heartfelt leaders, how can we hope to understand this in our very short careers? Hermes Trismegistus proposed seven rules to the universe that could shed some light on our connectivity, self-mastery, leadership response and life itself. The Hermetics were people who based their approach to life on his work.

Consider his seventh principle, as written in *The Kybalion* – the book of the Hermetic tenets: 'Gender is in everything. Everything has its masculine and feminine principles, and gender manifests on all planes.' In other words, there is a balance of masculine and feminine energy in everything we do, including who we are. Neither can exist without the other. In my experience, too much masculine energy without the feminine balance can lead to extreme bids for power and control over situations. Too much feminine energy without the balance of masculine can lead to short-term, emotionally driven responses. As heartfelt leaders, we learn to balance these energies over time as we iterate and learn from our experiences.

In every leader, there will be both masculine and feminine energies operating. These energies will play out in our moods, our responses, our ideas and our actions. As a heartfelt leader, you are challenged to give power to both serving your team and life itself.

Life was meant to be delightful

Following World War II, George Bernard Shaw wrote a series of plays in response to his frustration at the leadership of the day. He philosophised that the challenges of the modern world were so complex that we might all need to live longer lives so that we could apply our learning. In his preface to his series of plays, *Back to the Methuselah*, he wrote:

> *Life was not meant to be easy, my child, but take **courage**,*
> *for it can be **delightful**.*

Both Robert Kennedy, brother of the former president of the United States, and Malcolm Fraser, former prime minister of Australia, quoted Shaw's words. While Kennedy was misappropriated as the author, Fraser was condemned for using only the first part of the quote – 'Life was not meant to be easy' – as a patronising slur on the less fortunate. I think the full quote sums up the spirit of heartfelt leadership. Life is an iterative process. We keep learning, and in our learning, which can be challenging, comes our growth. If we dissect the Latin meaning of 'courage', the root of the word is *cor* – the Latin word for *heart*. Life was not meant to be easy, but take courage (and heart): it can be delightful.

You might be thinking, 'But I thought this book, *Heartfelt Leadership*, would make my life easier.' I contend *Heartfelt Leadership* will make your life better.

Activity 34: A heartfelt timeline

Reflect on your timeline that you created in the previous exercise. Now create another timeline – a lifetime timeline. Identify the times that you took courage and operated from your heart.

Grab a large piece of paper and a red marker. Draw a timeline and identify the key milestones in your own life – things like growing up, being at school, your first job, your first relationship, an incident that happened, buying a house, changing jobs and family events and circumstances. Then identify, by year or milestone, pivotal moments that happened. Think about all of those times that required courage. List what you learned from those events.

Again, consider the masculine and feminine traits you utilised. Which have you adopted in your leadership and life, and which could you adopt in your leadership to help to balance your energies in the future?

You might be saying, 'This is next level, Kerry. You're asking me to think about the times I've been brave.' Absolutely. As a heartfelt leader, you will ask more of yourself than anybody around you.

CONCLUSION

As heartfelt leaders, we learn, grow and develop best through iteration. We learn from our projects, our leadership endeavours and life. To understand and evolve as a heartfelt leader, you will need to be courageous with your energy and brave with your life.

As a heartfelt leader, you are constantly learning. The race will never end, but your performance will improve. If you don't invest in constant learning, you will adopt a leadership style that serves the short-term and says, 'What should I do right now to fix this problem?' versus, 'What can I do to grow my team, my business, myself?'

Embrace the learning journey, embrace the unknown and, most importantly, make yourself uncomfortable and step into your courage.

A heartfelt conclusion

Heartfelt Leadership is about **courage**, not control. It is also a practical model to get things done with a team. Heartfelt leadership will help you solve problems at work – problems with your people and your projects.

More importantly, heartfelt leadership is a growth philosophy that encourages you to find your truth and get honest about how you want to approach life.

Embracing heartfelt leadership will encourage you to examine how you approach leadership by asking you to consider both your masculine and feminine energies. Exploring these energies will take courage because heartfelt leadership is not a command-and-control solution – it is one of trusting that you have the depth of courage to lead.

Heartfelt leadership maps out nine principles that will support you to get more done with your team. These nine principles offer you a roadmap out of your day-to-day management pain and into a more courageous style of decision-making and leadership.

You may like to dip into the nine principles to solve immediate problems. Or, like some of my clients, you might like to adopt the principles in an orderly and logical fashion. I promise you that it will be worth it.

Most importantly, the nine principles will demand that you ask more of yourself, your heart and your courage than ever before. Together, the nine principles will demand that you know who you are and where you are going.

Adopting the nine principles as part of your leadership toolkit will mean that you will:

- get clear about what you want

- have a plan

- take responsibility for your own shit

- have difficult conversations

- choose your words

- keep it real for you and your team

- feed your team their favourite food

- celebrate life, because it is short

- know that life is an iterative process.

As you implement the heartfelt leadership principles you will become more aware of the complementary masculine and feminine skill sets including:

- **Results and creativity:** As a heartfelt leader you will need to get clear about what you want while balancing your creativity with results.

- **Planning and chaos:** If you're going somewhere great, you will need a solid plan, but also one that allows for some chaos and innovation.

- **Logic and intuition:** As you take responsibility for yourself and your leadership journey, the problem will never be about 'them' but about your perception of the problem. Allow both your intuition and your logic the space to do its work.

- **Tasks and relationships:** Having face-to-face conversations is all that really matters to a heartfelt leader. Conversations allow you to build relationships and make sure that tasks get done.

- **Direct and caring:** Getting things done matters. But, as a leader, your words matter a lot. Use them wisely to get things done in a way that releases you from doing them yourself.

- **Responsibility and innovation:** A lack of personal and team accountability lets us off the hook as heartfelt leaders. You will build responsibility into your leadership practice and balance it with innovation and fun.

- **Doing and sharing:** By communicating what your team wants to know, not what you want to be done, and you will create loyalty.

- **Legacy and reflection:** We are all going to be dead soon, so let's enjoy the ride and make sure that our legacy reflects who we indeed are.

- **Masculine and feminine:** Leadership and life are not linear processes. They get easier the more we do them, and we get better as we learn to balance our complementary energies for the greater good.

WHAT WILL LIFE BE LIKE AS A HEARTFELT LEADER?

As you implement the heartfelt principles and develop your heartfelt skill sets, your life as a leader will become richer and deeper, with less friction. You will be more focused because you'll know what you want and how you're going to get there. Little things and big things will not derail your plans because you'll have learned to anticipate and welcome chaos.

As a heartfelt leader, you will be in touch with your intuition and who you truly are. Your relationships will improve because of the genuine connections that you have with the people who matter. You will be more skilful in your language and better able to motivate your team to action through your improved focus on success. Your team members will clearly understand what they need to do to get things done, and won't be afraid to innovate or challenge the status quo.

With your newfound focus, you will understand the importance of celebration and the brevity of life. Your influence at home and work will outlive you, and you'll encourage those who follow to model your approach.

Finally, as a heartfelt leader, you'll become comfortable with the discomfort and step into your future with a heart full of courage.

FINAL HEARTFELT THOUGHTS

I am a heartfelt leader work-in-progress. Like you, I find it hard to get the balance right. Perhaps the biggest obstacle in leaping to becoming a heartfelt leader will be the voice in your head. You might be concerned about not having all of the answers because trusting your team looks pretty risky right now.

You might also lack the courage to make the shift right now because you feel uncomfortable in this new leadership style. Or you might not feel like you have the necessary emotional or technical skills yet.

Like learning any new skill, all of these concerns are real and valid. The best way to overcome them is by starting small with daily practice. A daily reflection in your journal can help immensely in contemplating and recording your progress.

In your transition into a heartfelt leader, you may feel like me – uncomfortable. But while I think this way, I know in my heart that this is my responsibility. I often think of my favourite quote, from Jennifer Granholm:

> *Leadership is to plant trees under whose shade*
> *I shall never sit.*

Leaving a legacy of leaders (and trees) drives me, personally and practically. My personal ambition is to plant a million trees in my lifetime. Annually, I plant around a thousand trees. I've been doing this since my 20s. I believe that this is an example of a vast and lasting powerful measure of what we could collectively do together, just like each of us adopting a more heartfelt approach to leadership.

I would love to hear from you if this book has inspired you in any way or you'd like to continue the conversation. If you do connect with me, I will plant a tree in your honour simply because I'd love to have a chat with you about heartfelt leadership. Would you please reach out to me if I can help?

To again quote George Bernard Shaw,

> *You see things; and you say 'why?' But I dream things*
> *that never were; and I say, 'Why not?'*

My wish is that, universally, every person who wishes to lead a movement, a family, an organisation or a country finds their version of heartfelt courage to do so.

References

Introduction
Viktor Frankl 1946, *Man's Search for Meaning*, Beacon Press.

Principle 1
Greg Behrendt and Liz Tuccillo 2004, *He's Just Not That Into You: The No-Excuses Truth to Understanding Guys*, Simon Spotlight Entertainment.
Edith Eger 2017, *The Choice: Embrace the Possible*, Scribner Book Company.

Principle 2
Brendon Burchard, brendon.com.

Principle 4
Kim Scott 2017, *Radical Candor: Be a Kick-Ass Boss Without Losing Your Humanity*, St Martin's Press.

Principle 9
Three Initiates 1908, *The Kybalion: A Study of the Hermetic Philosophy of Ancient Egypt and Greece,* The Yogi Publication Society.
George Bernard Shaw 1921, *Back to Methuselah (A Metabiological Pentateuch)*, Constable.

About the author

Kerry Swan is a born-and-bred project manager. With more than 20 years' experience as a self-employed consultant, coach and teacher, Kerry has worked with hundreds of managers and leaders. For most of that time, Kerry taught project management and provided strategic business planning advice and management consulting services to organisations large and small.

Kerry is also an entrepreneur. Having survived two business start-ups and the volatility of business in the wake of the Covid-19 pandemic, Kerry understands, personally, the realities and frustrations of business and leading a team through change.

These days Kerry works with her husband Craig across their three diverse family businesses. With business interests in real estate, earthmoving and agribusiness and a team of more than 35 people, Kerry loves the daily challenges of leadership.

Kerry has a hands-on love of the propagation and revegetation of Australian native trees. In their spare time, Kerry and her family plant 1000 trees annually on their family farm on the beautiful Narrung Peninsula in South Australia.